Income and Value Measurement

**The Chapman & Hall Series in Accounting and Finance**

*Consulting editors*
John Perrin, Emeritus Professor of the University of Warwick and Price
Waterhouse Fellow in Public Sector Accounting at the University of Exeter;
Richard M. S. Wilson, Professor of Management Control in the School of
Finance and Information at the Queen's University of Belfast and L. C. L.
Skerratt, Professor of Financial Accounting at the University of
Manchester.

H. M. Coombs and D. E. Jenkins
**Public Sector Financial Management**

J. C. Drury
**Management and Cost Accounting (2nd edn)**
(Also available: **Students' Manual, Teachers' Manual**)

C. R. Emmanuel, D. T. Otley and K Merchant
**Accounting for Management Control (2nd edn)**
(Also Available: **Teachers' Manual**)

C. R. Emmanuel, D. T. Otley and K. Merchant (editors)
**Readings in Accounting for Management Control**

D. Henley, C. Holtham, A. Likierman and J. Perrin
**Public Sector Accounting and Financial Control (3rd edn)**

R. C. Laughlin and R. H. Gray
**Financial Accounting: method and meaning**
(Also available: **Teachers' Guide**)

G. A. Lee
**Modern Financial Accounting (4th edn)**
(Also available: **Solutions Manual**)

T. A. Lee
**Income and Value Measurement (3rd edn)**

T. A. Lee
**Company Financial Reporting (2nd edn)**

T. A. Lee
**Cash Flow Accounting**

S. P. Lumby
**Investment Appraisal and Financing Decisions (4th edn)**
(Also available: **Students' Manual**)

A. G. Puxty and J. C. Dodds
**Financial Management: method and meaning (2nd edn)**
(Also available: **Teachers' Guide**)

J. M. Samuels, F. M. Wilkes and R. E. Brayshaw
**Management of Company Finance (5th edn)**
(Also available: **Students' Manual**)

B. C. Williams and B. J. Spaul
**IT and Accounting: The impact of information technology**

R. M. S. Wilson and Wai Fong Chua
**Managerial Accounting: method and meaning**
(Also available: **Teachers' Guide**)

# Income and Value Measurement

## Theory and Practice

Third edition

T. A. Lee
Culverhouse Professor of Accountancy

Culverhouse School of
Accountancy, University of Alabama

**CHAPMAN & HALL**
University and Professional Division
London · Glasgow · New York · Tokyo · Melbourne · Madras

to my parents

**Published by Chapman & Hall, 2-6 Boundary Row, London SE1 8HN**

Chapman & Hall, 2-6 Boundary Row, London SE1 8HN, UK

Blackie Academic & Professional, Wester Cleddens Road, Bishopbriggs, Glasgow G64 2NZ, UK

Chapman & Hall, 29 West 35th Street, New York NY10001, USA

Chapman & Hall Japan, Thomson Publishing Japan, Hirakawacho Nemoto Building, 6F, 1-7-11 Hirakawa-cho, Chiyoda-ku, Tokyo 102, Japan

Chapman & Hall Australia, Thomas Nelson Australia, 102 Dodds Street, South Melbourne, Victoria 3205, Australia

Chapman & Hall India, R. Seshadri, 32 Second Main Road, CIT East, Madras 600 035, India

First edition 1974
Reprinted 1977, 1978, 1978
Second edition 1980
Reprinted 1981, 1982(twice), 1983
Third edition 1985
Reprinted 1986, 1987, 1989, 1990, 1991, 1992, 1993

© 1974, 1980, 1985 T.A. Lee

Printed in Great Britain by St Edmundsbury Press Ltd, Bury St Edmunds, Suffolk

ISBN 0 412 38180 X

A catalogue record for this book is available from the British Library
Library of Congress Cataloging-in-Publication Data available

# Preface

A winter of discontent has existed in the area of income and value measurement since the writing of the second edition of this text. Due to the continuing debate on price-level accounting generally, and current cost accounting particularly, there appears to be little agreement on these issues in practice. This makes an understanding of the underlying conceptional framework an essential requirement for practitioners, students and teachers alike. The relevance of the text has therefore been enhanced. However, one problem which has arisen is that the nature of so-called 'inflation accounting' practice is changing as the debate about it proceeds. Mention of particular practices in a text such as this can rapidly make it appear outdated.

With this in mind, the opportunity has been taken to 'neutralize' the text in this repect – that is, only to use specific practices as a means of illustrating a particular model. In this case, use has been made of the principles contained in *Statement of Standard Accounting Practice 16* (1980) to illustrate current cost accounting; and *Provisional Statement of Standard Accounting Practice 7* (1974) to illustrate general price-level adjustments. Both of these *Statements* are redundant in practice but, nevertheless, contain general principles which are of much longer duration. By removing all mention of current practices from the text, and only using important past pronouncements for illustration, the text hopefully will have a more timeless quality than hitherto – thus making it easier to use for teaching purposes.

The final chapter also contains an up-to-date account of the writer's thoughts on cash flow accounting, and the Selected Bibliography is a very much restricted choice of readings to aid students and teachers. The literature of income and value measurement has become so large that it is now counter-productive to produce the complete bibliographies of the previous editions.

## Preface to the second edition

The first edition of this book was written in 1972 and published in 1974, shortly before the continuing debate on so-called inflation accounting ensued. Originally conceived as a theoretical text, it has increasingly gained a professional audience, thus making it of relevance to students and practitioners alike. In this context, it is interesting to observe that matters of apparently only theoretical importance in 1972 became topics of great practical relevance in 1979. The area of income and value measurement is no longer the exclusive preserve of the academic accountant or economist. Matters such as holding gains, current values, capital maintenance, and borrowing gains are as much part of the vocabulary of the practising accountant as they are of the lecturer. It has taken only a handful of years for this situation to arise.

It is comforting to note that most of the text has withstood the test of time. The major part of its content remains as relevant and valid today as when it was first written. However, five years of use of the book, together with the previously mentioned inflation accounting debate, have required the text to be amended and supplemented. In particular, the following matters have received attention: *(a)* a greater attention to user needs and objectives and to attendant information criteria; *(b)* an improved computation and explanation of economic income and value as applied to the business entity (including relevant general price-level adjustments); *(c)* extended coverage of the nature of replacement cost holding gains; *(d)* an improved computation and explanation of realizable income and its relationship to business income; *(e)* an additional chapter on mixed values and current cost accounting; *(f)* additional explanations of general price-level adjustments; *(g)* an alternative closing chapter on the validity of the income concept; and *(h)* a greatly expanded bibliography.

Such changes have arisen as a result of several influences: the use of the book over several years by numerous students, reviews of it in academic journals, and comments from colleagues. Of particular help have been comments from Professor A. Barton (Australian National University), Professor P. Bird (University of Kent at Canterbury), and Professor R. H. Parker (University of Exeter). Not all the suggestions have been implemented – some are matters of either judgement or personal preference; others would require an extension of the book beyond its present remit. Hopefully, the text will therefore contain items which continue to cause argument and debate. Unless this is the case, the book will be failing in its stated objective – to provide its reader with material with which he or she can pursue the income and value measurement debate.

## Acknowledgements to the first edition

No textbook is ever written without guidance and comment from various persons and, at times, it is extremely difficult to identify all who have been involved in this process. Therefore, to all such students and colleagues who go unmentioned, humble apologies and grateful thanks. The main debt of gratitude, however, is to Professor Andrew McCosh of the Manchester Business School (for providing the initial opportunity for writing the book and for comments on early drafts); to Professor Geoffrey Whittington of the University of Edinburgh (for not only commenting on several drafts but also for putting up with numerous arguments on the text with this 'dour Scotsman'); and to Debbie Hathorn, Chris Nash, and Peter Ford for making the unreadable readable. Any errors remaining are, of course, the responsibility of the author.

# Contents

# Introduction

'Annual income twenty pounds, annual expenditure nineteen nineteen six, result happiness. Annual income twenty pounds, annual expenditure twenty pounds ought and six, result misery.'

The above well-known quotation from Dickens's *David Copperfield* characterizes, albeit indirectly, two fundamentally different conceptions of income. First, that of the accountant, who traditionally measures it in terms of a residue of revenues over expenditure; and secondly, that of the economist, who describes it, in part at least, as a psychological state of personal enjoyment and satisfaction. The literature of accountancy and economics bears ample witness to the significance placed upon the concept by each profession. Yet, with one or two notable exceptions,[1] the subject has never been explored extensively on an inter-disciplinary basis. The main aim of this book is therefore to examine, in detail and as simply as possible, the concept and measurement of income and its related concepts of capital and value so as to reflect the approaches of both accountant and economist.

The concept of income is a familiar topic. It is the focal point for much financial accounting theory and practice; it forms a substantial part of both micro and macro-economic thought; and it is a primary motivating force in business management. Accountants have traditionally measured and analysed income from the point of view of the business entity and its proprietors, whereas economists have usually examined it, in its micro-economic sense, from the point of view of the individual consumer. This has led to the differences in approach and methodology which subsequent chapters will highlight and examine.

Canning[2] has been generally accepted as the first major inter-disciplinary contributor to date in this area, with Edwards,[3] Alexander,[4] Edwards and Bell,[5] Solomons,[6] Chambers,[7] Sterling,[8] and Barton[9] also providing useful inter-disciplinary studies. Canning, however, wrote his book in 1929, and limited his analysis to the economic and traditional accounting concepts of income. Since then, particularly during the 1960s, a third school of thought has been established which advocates current value income. This book therefore incorporates and examines the latter concept in detail, contrasting it with the traditional accounting and economic concepts.

The main reason for writing this book has been prompted by a growing debate between accountants, financial analysts, stockbrokers, investors and politicians, concerning the rather high number of faults present in the traditional accounting concept of income: for example, the flexibility of its measurement practices, the assumed stability of the purchasing power of the monetary measuring unit, and a widespread failure to recognize various contemporary values and value changes. It is apparent, also, that a growing number of accountants and economists are interested in attempting to ensure that the operational accounting income concept is at least compatible with economic thinking, while retaining as many favourable features of traditional accounting as possible – hence, the emergence of the current value school of thought. It therefore seems timely to compare and contrast these various ideas – particularly at a time when accountants in practice are debating and implementing them as alternatives to those of traditional accounting.

The several major objectives of the book are, in summary, (a) to explain fully income and capital in both accounting and economic terms; (b) to describe the various accounting and economic income measurements; (c) to explain the fundamental problems of capital, value and capital maintenance common to each measurement model; (d) to compare and contrast each of these various models; and (e), from this comparison, to describe significant similarities and dissimilarities in accounting and economic thinking. The book will also discuss recent developments in the practice of income and value measurement, and should therefore be of interest to students of both accounting and economics, while presupposing a minimal understanding of generally accepted financial accounting principles and introductory economics (including the basic terminology of these two disciplines). The contents of the book are, however, concerned only with 'micro-economic' income and do not deal with National Income. This exclusion is made to simplify the comparisons of accounting and economic concepts.

The outline of the book is as follows:

*Chapter 1* deals with the fundamental definitions and explanations of income, capital, value, and capital maintenance, thus giving a broad introduction to most of the topics to be explained in greater detail in later chapters. It also explains in outline the unique but confusing role of price-level adjustments.

*Chapter 2* describes the nature and purpose of income determination, as well as the main information and communication criteria which should govern its measurement.

*Chapter 3* describes the various economic income concepts under conditions of certainty and uncertainty. In particular, Hicks's[10] concept of 'welloffness' is fully discussed, including its adaptation to the business entity. This should provide the theoretical basis for subsequent explanations and comparisons with the various accounting measurement models.

*Chapter 4* analyses the traditional accounting concept of income based upon historic cost, before contrasting it with the theoretical economic model.

*Chapter 5* explains, in general terms, the current value concept of income which has been advocated as a reasoned compromise between the traditional accounting model and the Hicksian economic model as applied to the business entity.

*Chapter 6* expands the content and analysis of the previous chapter by examining the current value entry model based upon replacement or current cost. In particular, it utilises a computational format based on Edwards and Bell's[11] concept of business income, comparing this with the traditional accounting concept of income.

*Chapter 7* describes the alternative current value model based upon exit prices – i.e. net realizable values or current cash equivalents, as advocated by Chambers[12] and Sterling.[13] The concept of realizable income is contrasted with the concepts of business income and traditional accounting income.

*Chapter 8* outlines the mixed value model which has been applied in various countries. Based on Bonbright's[14] 'value to the owner', it describes and discusses the major principles of current cost accounting.

*Chapter 9* presents a comparative analysis of the three current value based income models, as described in Chapters 6, 7 and 8, and the economic income model, as described in Chapter 3.

*Chapter 10* relaxes the assumption of monetary stability which is kept to throughout Chapters 3 to 9 inclusive, and examines the nature of price changes, contrasting general, specific and relative price-level adjustments. The application of general price-level adjustments to each of the main accounting and economic income models is described.

*Chapter 11* discusses the validity of the income concept as measurable and reportable financial information, and considers an alternative information concept – cash flow accounting.

Each chapter is supported by its own section in the Selected Bibliography which follows at the end of the text, and this should allow the reader to study individual topics in greater depth. The selection has been made on the grounds of relevance, conciseness and readability.

It should be noted that the term 'income' is used throughout the text and is synonymous with the alternative terms of 'profit' and 'earnings' which are so often used in accounting practice. As this is an interdisciplinary text, 'income' is felt to be the one term which is likely to be generally accepted by accountants and economists alike. The term 'profit', particularly, has an accounting meaning which differs from that normally attributed to it by the economist. 'Income', on the other hand, is a less restrictive term which is capable of encompassing all measured profits and gains recognized by either the accountant or the economist.

In addition, the term 'business entity' used throughout this and later chapters should be taken (unless otherwise instructed) as synonymous with the organisation to which income can be attributed rather than the entity concept which relates to the way in which such income is to be reported in terms of the various vested interests in the organisation.

Finally, the reader should note that the complex but supplementary question of taxation in income measurement has been ignored throughout the text, on the grounds of simplicity; and that a stable monetary unit has been assumed throughout Chapters 3 to 9, inclusive, again in order to simplify the discussion of fundamentals. The latter assumption is, however, relaxed in Chapter 10.

### References

1. For example, J. B. Canning, *The Economics of Accountancy*, The Ronald Press, 1929; E. O. Edwards and P. W. Bell, *The Theory and Measurement of Business Income*, University of California Press, 1961; R. J. Chambers, *Accounting, Evaluation and Economic Behaviour*, Prentice-Hall, 1966; and R. R. Sterling, *Theory of the Measurement of Enterprise Income*, University of Kansas Press, 1970.

2. Canning, *The Economics of Accountancy*.

3. R. S. Edwards, 'The Nature and Measurement of Income', thirteen weekly articles in *The Accountant*, 1938.

4. S. Alexander, 'Income Measurement in a Dynamic Economy', *Five Monographs on Business Income*, American Institute of Accountants, 1948.

5. Edwards and Bell, *The Theory and Measurement of Business Income*.

6. D. Solomons, 'Economic and Accounting Concepts of Income', *Accounting Review*, July 1961, pp. 374–83.

7. Chambers, *Accounting, Evaluation and Economic Behaviour*.

8. Sterling, *Theory of the Measurement of Enterprise Income*.

9. A. D. Barton, 'An Analysis of Business Income Concepts', *ICRA Occasional Paper 7*, 1975.

10. J. R. Hicks, *Value and Capital*, Clarendon Press, 2nd edition, 1946, pp. 171–81.

11. Edwards and Bell, *The Theory and Measurement of Business Income*.

12. Chambers, *Accounting, Evaluation and Economic Behaviour*.

13. Sterling, *Theory of the Measurement of Enterprise Income*.

14. J. C. Bonbright, *The Valuation of Property*, McGraw Hill, 1937, p. 71.

# 1 Nature and relationship of income, capital and value

## The nature of income

Despite its prominence in accounting thought, it is surprising to find so little of the relevant literature devoted to fundamental expositions of the nature of income. In contrast, the literature of micro-economics contains a great deal of discussion on this topic, and therefore much of the material in this chapter is drawn from the work of economists.

As was inferred in the Introduction, the accountant has traditionally defined income as a surplus arising from business activity, resulting from the cash-to-cash cycle of business operations and derived from a periodic matching of revenues from sales with relevant costs. Thus he describes income in terms of the business entity and its economic activity in a defined past period of time. Accounting income is therefore an *ex post* measure – i.e. measured 'after the event'.

The matching process is an integral part of the accounting income determination function, and causes an aggregation of unallocated costs to be carried forward at the end of each defined accounting period; these costs represent the non-monetary assets of the entity, such as buildings, plant and inventories. Such asset measurements, together with corresponding measurements of the entity's monetary resources, and after deduction of its various liabilities, give rise to its residual equity or accounting capital. The traditional accounting balance sheet is the accepted vehicle for reporting these various related historic measures.

Accounting income ($Y_a$) is therefore a measure which results in a corresponding measure of capital ($R$). Indeed, it can be identified with the periodic movement in such capital; i.e. $Y_a = R_t - R_{t-1}$; where $R_t$ is the residual equity at the end of the period, and $R_{t-1}$ is the residual equity at the beginning of the period; assuming no new capital or loan receipts or payments, no dividends, and a constant price-level. If a dividend had been paid to the owners of the entity, $Y_a$ would then identify with $D+(R_t-R_{t-1})$; where D represents the dividend. In other words, $R_t$ would be computed after payment of the dividend, and $R_t-R_{t-1}$ would be the undistributed portion of $Y_a$ for the defined period.

Accounting income is therefore a residual measure, and is conceived as a comparison of business accomplishment and effort in a past period.[1] It is also a temporal measure, normally computed in terms of matching revenue and expenditure transactions, although it can be analysed as a temporal change in capital (as above). It is also a predominantly historical measure of business activity, looking back in time and identifying and equating past efforts and accomplishments; and generally being accepted by the business community as a measure of an entity's operational success or failure.

The economist's view of the nature of income is somewhat different, the main difference being its conception as a personal rather than an entity measure. Indeed, one economist, Fisher,[2] has stated that an entity, not being a human being, cannot have income. However, several economists,[3] in contrast to the views of Fisher, have adapted the economist's concept of personal income to the business entity, and this will be dealt with in Chapter 3.

Fisher[4] is widely regarded as the founding father of contemporary economic thinking on the nature of personal income.[5] He described it as a series of perceived events or psychic experiences called enjoyment. Enjoyment came from the consumption of goods and services, and income was a monetary measure of this personal consumption. Fisher did not recognize increases in capital as income, for, in his view, such saving was potential consumption from which no current psychic enjoyment could be derived. He therefore omitted saving from his income identity. On the other hand, when consumption included a return of capital, Fisher identified such disinvestment as part of personal income because it was consumed and enjoyed.

Later economists have not entirely followed Fisher's strictly psychological conception of income, but have rather identified personal economic income $(Y_e)$ as consumption plus saving; i.e. $Y_e = C+S$; where C represents consumption, and S represents saving, generally interpreted as the periodic change in personal economic capital (K). Therefore personal economic income is normally identified as $Y_e = C+(K_t-K_{t-1})$; where $K_t$ is the economic capital at the end of the period, and $K_{t-1}$ is the economic capital at the beginning of the period. In contrast to traditional accounting, the economist therefore computes capital so as to measure income.

Hicks[6] developed the earlier conceptions of Fisher into a generally accepted theory of economic income. He presented his concept of 'welloffness' as the basis for a rough approximation of personal income. He defined income, expanding on the aforementioned identities of $Y_e = C+S = C+(K_t-K_{t-1})$, as the maximum which can be consumed by a person in a defined period without impairing his 'welloffness' as it existed at the beginning of the period. 'Welloffness', for the purposes of this section, is equivalent to wealth or capital. For example (postulating constant prices), if an individual's cash receipts for a period are £500, with his capital £1,000 at the beginning of the period and £800 at the end of it, then $Y_e = £500+(800-1,000) = £300$. Therefore, although £500 could be consumed by the individual, the maximum which he should consume is £300, if his capital is to be maintained at £1,000. £200 of the £500 realised cash flow figure is a possible return of capital. If possible consumption is £500, with beginning capital at £800 and end capital at £1,000, then $Y_e = £500+(1,000-800) = £700$; i.e. £700 could be consumed by the individual without impairing his opening capital of £800. Hicks thus highlighted the importance of the concept of capital maintenance in income determination, and, indeed, his reasoning can be seen in his fuller definition of income as the maximum a person can consume in a period and still be able to expect the same level of consumption in the next period. C, therefore, in the aforementioned identity of $Y_e = C+(K_t-K_{t-1})$, should be redefined as the expected or actual cash realizations in the given circumstances rather than as the level of consumption identified as income. The definition of C as realized cash flows will therefore be adopted throughout this book.

Following the Fisher-Hicks tradition, therefore, economists[7] appear to be generally agreed about the nature of measured personal income: first, that psychological wants and satisfactions underlie it; secondly, that it is made up of two components, consumption and saving; and thirdly, that it exists only after opening capital has been maintained. This being so, there does appear to be some superficial similarity between the accountant's and economist's conceptions of income – i.e. the previously defined accounting identity $Y_a = D+(R_t-R_{t-1})$ as compared with the economic identity $Y_e = C+(K_t-K_{t-1})$. However, although both are capital based, there are significant differences in the measurements attributable to R and K capitals, as later chapters will specify more clearly, and there are also differences in the approaches to measurement – the accountant measuring income with capital as a residue, and the economist measuring capital with income as a residue. It should also be remembered that, in a micro-economic sense, the accountant's concept of income is an entity one; whereas the economist's is intended as a personal one.

## The nature of capital

Accounting capital is normally described in terms of the residual equity of a business entity, and is identified with its various assets net of any corresponding liabilities. These assets can be divided into monetary and non-monetary categories, and accounting capital is therefore traditionally conceived as a collection of available physical or tangible goods and services expressed in aggregate money terms. Capital is, in this sense, simply an expression of the entity's property rights in net assets. As Canning[8] has stated, accountants therefore tend to regard assets as physical or tangible objects symbolizing future service potential rather than as service potential from which future income can be derived. The result is that accounting capital is mainly transactions based, derived from the process of determining income from recorded transactions. Consequently, it is a measure depending entirely on the nature of the transactions recorded. In many respects, it is far removed from the economist's conception of capital.

As with income, much of the economic thought supporting the concept of capital is derived from the Fisher-Hicks tradition, and is conceived in personal rather than entity terms. Fisher[9] regarded capital as a stock embodying future services, with income as the flow from this stock. Following this line of thought, economists normally look forward in time in terms of anticipated services, and these expectations form the basis of determining economic capital.

Fisher thus regarded capital as the present value of future anticipated benefits, as represented in the equation

$$K_0 = \sum_{t=1}^{n} C_t(1+i)^{-t}$$

where $K_0$ represents capital at the point of time $t = 0$, C represents anticipated future consumption in terms of predicted cash flows, and i represents the subjective personal rate of interest (a personal opportunity cost rate). Most economists would agree with this conception of personal capital, particularly its valuation in terms of discounted future benefits. Both Fisher[10] and Lindahl[11] described it as wealth, without much further definition, although each accepted its existence and relationship to saving and income. Hicks,[12] on the other hand, described it as 'welloffness' and defined this as the capitalized money value of prospective receipts. He was here, however, attempting to get away from the traditional Fisher approach to capital as a stock, income as a flow, and the rate of interest as the bridge between the two. He felt this latter view gave too much of an impression of capital and income being separate concepts, and of capital being a collection of physical goods and services. His view was that capital was a future stream of income symbolizing the latter's present value – in other words, that capital and income were really one and the same concept, although they had to be isolated for measurement purposes.

Summarizing, therefore, it seems that the major difference between accountants and economists is one of measurement as highlighted by Boulding;[13] that accountants measure capital in terms of actualities, as the primary by-product of the accounting income measurement process; and that economists measure it in terms of potentialities, in order to measure economic income. Despite this, the accountant and the economist would almost certainly agree on two points: first, that capital is an essential ingredient in income determination; and secondly, that it involves measurement and valuation procedures.

## The relationship of income and capital

Although not specifically emphasized, the two preceding sections on income and capital have touched on the fundamental relationship between the two topics. In accounting, capital and income are regarded widely as a stock and a flow, with the stock resulting from a transacted flow which is accounted for when measuring accounting income. In economics, the stock-flow concept also exists, though the generally accepted relationship appears to be the valuation of capital as a discounted future stream of income, and the measurement of income as an expired portion of such capital.

A rigorous examination of the relationship between income and capital was first made by Fisher.[14] He regarded interest as the bridge between the two concepts; i.e. as the price of hiring money today in order to obtain a certain amount of money tomorrow. This may be represented in the simple identity

$$K_0 = \frac{K_1}{(1+i)} \quad \text{or} \quad i = \frac{K_1 - K_0}{K_0}$$

where $K_0$ is capital at the point of time $t = 0$; $K_1$ is capital at the point of time $t = 1$, and i is the fixed rate of interest at which K is invested. However, Fisher confined his analysis to this fixed-interest security type of situation where $K_0$ and i are known with certainty or where $K_0$

and $K_1$ are known with certainty and i is the computed internal rate of return. But, as Hicks[15] pointed out, this is a special case, and does not really relate to most 'real world' situations, where i varies over time and where K is based on a series of predictions which can also vary over time. Hicks therefore preferred to treat the interest rate simply as the discount factor necessary to value capital in terms of anticipated income. (The problems of varying interest rates or discount factors and varying expectations of income in a world of uncertainty will be explained in Chapter 3, and will show that the Fisher income-capital model reflects an unreal world of perfect knowledge and certainty.)

## The concept of capital maintenance

The previous discussion of the nature of income and capital has also highlighted the crucial role played by the concept of capital maintenance in the process of measuring periodic income – i.e. opening capital must be maintained before there can be recognition of such income. However, this begs numerous questions as to what capital should be maintained – should it be money capital (as is the case with traditional accounting); physical capital (i.e. in terms of tangible assets or operating capability); potential consumption (as expressed by economists in discounted cash flow measurements); or purchasing power (as suggested in certain recent inflation accounting proposals)?

Numerous combinations of these alternatives are possible, and the main ones will be discussed, where relevant, in different parts of this text. Meanwhile, it is sufficient to note that the idea of capital and its maintenance is entirely dependent on the definition of capital used, and that there are a number of alternative definitions from which to choose. Much depends on the valuation system adopted.

## The concept of value

So far, the superficial similarity of accounting and economic incomes has been shown: accounting income being previously identified and defined as $D+(R_t-R_{t-1})$, economic income being previously identified and defined as $C+(K_t-K_{t-1})$, and both, therefore, involving computations of capital. The fundamental difference, however, is not so apparent. This concerns the values attributed to both capital R and capital K, and the purpose of this section is to examine more closely the role of valuation in income determination, and the nature of the differences in values attributable to accounting and economic capitals.

It is generally accepted, by accountants and economists, that the value placed upon capital determines the particular measure of income – i.e. different capital values in either of the previously mentioned income identities will produce different income figures. Indeed, in Lindahl's[16] view, income is a concept of value. Ijiri[17] also supports this relatively self-evident observation, when he states that it can be the same physical goods, services and economic activity underlying different capital and income measures, which are made to vary because of the application of different value bases.

Value implies appraising or prizing some object or concept either in ethical terms (reflecting the moral attributes of the object or concept) or in economic terms (reflecting choice, preference or willingness to sacrifice). Valuation, therefore, is the process of ranking these attributes or preferences. With regard to scarce economic resources, in which accountants and economists are interested when determining income and capital, the concept of value and the process of valuation are pertinent, particularly when expressed in economic terms.

In an economic sense, as mentioned above, valuation involves the measurement of choices, preferences or sacrifices. These sacrifices are temporal in nature, and so it is possible to measure past, present or future sacrifices in terms of past, present or future values. Indeed, it is possible to find all three types of value in both the accounting and economic concepts of income and capital. For example, the typical financial accounting balance sheet contains past values in terms of historic costs, as well as estimations of present and future values, particularly in the areas of fixed asset and inventory accounting; and economic models are based upon projections of the future as well as present or past consumption figures.

The common valuing agent in both accounting and economics is recognized as money – it is measurable, and employs an accepted scale which is additive. It also has the distinct advantage of reflecting economic choice, preference or sacrifice because of its general command over goods and services. It is a primary measuring agent which can acquire goods and services with a greater marginal utility with regard to money outlay than is attributable to the goods and services currently held. As Sterling[18] points out, this is extremely important in connection with the topic of value and valuation, because value only has significance to the accountant and the economist when there are uncompleted economic resource exchanges – i.e when the resources underlying capital are in non-monetary form; thereby reflecting choice and utility. Thus, the main accounting and economic problem in this area is applying relevant values to the appropriate economic resources underlying capital.

Traditional accounting is mainly based upon past values for relevant resources, in terms of historic costs, although certain current values are incorporated, together with certain estimations of future values. In addition, as later chapters will describe, there are advocates of accounting concepts of income and capital using current values for resources. However, despite its obvious and logical connection with income and capital, accountants have been loath to become involved in accounting for value. As Sprouse[19] stated, this is a highly personal and sensitive term which accountants have tended to disregard. Indeed, many accountants have written that, because of the personal nature of values, which imply estimation and subjective judgement, accountants should not become valuers, but should, instead, continue to limit their activities to reporting factual transactions and historic costs. Because of this attitude, MacNeal[20] has warned accountants that, despite their reluctance to value resources, their financial reports describing income and capital imply, in a misleading way, that some form of valuation process has taken place in connection with the resources underlying capital.

The economic income model, in all its various forms, values capital on the basis of discounted future net cash receipts. Because of the necessary prediction of future cash flows for discounting purposes, as well as the choice of an appropriate discount rate, much of the economic approach to income and capital is founded on subjective judgement and estimation, from which are derived values which the accountant, traditionally an advocate of objective and verifiable measurements, finds hard to accept as feasible and valid for financial reporting purposes. Nevertheless, as the work of Hicks[21] reveals, the economist is interested in measuring past, present and future values for capital, for he considers three different incomes (the detail and computation of each of which will be dealt with in Chapter 3); i.e. (a) $Y_e = C + (K_t - K_{t-1})$ which is described as ideal income and represents a world of perfect knowledge and certainty where future flows, interest rates and values are known; (b) $Y_e = C' + (K'_t - K_{t-1})$ which is described as income *ex ante* and represents a world of uncertainty and imperfect knowledge where future flows, interest rates and values are largely a matter of subjective judgement and prediction (as this is income measured 'before the event' – i.e. at the beginning of the relevant period – $C'$ is the anticipated realized cash flow of the period, $K'_t$ is the anticipated capital value capital value at the end of the period but measured at the beginning of the period, and $K_{t-1}$ is the capital value at the beginning of the period and measured at that point of time); and (c) $Y_e = C + (K_t - K'_{t-1})$ which is described as income *ex post* and again represents the world of uncertainty and imperfect knowledge (as this is income measured 'after the event' – i.e. at the end of the relevant period – C is known, but $K_t$ is the capital value at the end of the period and measured at that point of time, and $K'_{t-1}$ is the capital value at the beginning of the period, measured at the end of the period, and thus revised for any changes in former expectations during the period). It should be noted by way of comparison that, although income *ex post* is measured after the event, it still involves uncertainty and imperfect knowledge because capital must be valued at the end of the period of measurement on the basis of future expectations in an imperfect world. This contrasts with the ideal income model, where future expectations and capital values are known with certainty because a perfect world is assumed.

Each of the above concepts of income, with the exception of the somewhat unrealistic ideal income, involves prediction and subjective value because capital K is based always on the value of future benefits. They are, therefore, totally different from the traditional accounting approach to income, capital and value. MacNeal[22] has described this difference as, essentially, one of valuation – the accountant basing his concept of income upon market transactions and prices; and the economist basing his concept upon philosophical-psychological judgements and predictions. Canning[23] described the difference as the accountant concerning himself with 'direct' values derivable from market forces, and the economist concerning himself with 'indirect' values derived through subjective judgements.

Accounting values are therefore normally market rather than psychologically based. They can be divided up into two main groups: historic and current values. Historic values of the resources underlying capital form the basis of the generally accepted traditional accounting income; i.e. income involving measurements of past acquisition costs and reflecting economic sacrifices at the relevant acquisition dates rather than at the subsequent dates of accounting and reporting. Such costs are past values, but only coincidently are they contemporary values. Current values, on the other hand, are resource values established at the time of accounting and reporting income, and therefore reflect present sacrifices. They fall into two categories: first, entry value or replacement cost describing the current cost of replacing an economic resource of the reporting entity; and secondly, exit value or net realizable value representing 'opportunity cost' (the value of a resource in its next best alternative form). Each of these accounting values will be discussed in greater detail later (Chapter 6, 7 and 8), in connection with the income and capital concepts to which they relate;

and each will be compared with the future-based economic concept of value represented by discounted future net receipts.

## The separate roles of valuation and capital maintenance

The earlier sections have described separately the relationship of capital maintenance and valuation to income. It is now important to pinpoint the difference between capital maintenance and valuation. The concept of capital maintenance is a vital part of income determination because of the need to incorporate in the income computation a measure of the change in capital during the relevant period. Value, on the other hand, is a necessary ingredient in the computation of capital to which the capital maintenance concept is then applied in determining income. Both are therefore necessary to the income determination process, but neither can of itself measure income.

## The price-level problem, capital maintenance and income

Up to this point, income determination has been described with the assumption that value and capital changes over time have been due entirely to operational activity, demand and supply market forces, or changes in expectations. In other words, the relevant capital maintenance process has been explained as a straightforward comparison of opening and closing capital. However, this assumes the temporal stability of the value of the monetary unit used in measuring capital; i.e. the generalized purchasing power of the relevant monetary unit is deemed to remain constant over time. But money is a means of exchange, and therefore it has a known and variable value over time in relation to goods and services generally. For example, in times of inflation, when the market price of a particular good rises, this may be due to its economic value rising in relation to other goods and services as well as to a fall in the general purchasing power of the monetary unit of exchange. For example, if 10 units of a good A were acquired at $t_1$ for £100, and at $t_2$ the total acquisition cost for a similar 10 units was £110, it may not be the case that the goods concerned are regarded by the market as being 10 per cent more valuable in relation to other goods. If the prices of all goods and services have risen on average between $t_1$ and $t_2$ by 5 per cent, due to inflation, then £5 of the value increase could be said to be inflationary and the remaining £5 could be properly described as due to market forces putting a higher value on the goods concerned. In income determination, these general principles can be applied to temporal changes in accounting or economic capital. In other words, part of the change in the value of capital used in computing income may be inflationary because of a fall in the general power of the monetary unit.

The problem of price-level changes has been recognized in writings relating to each of the alternative accounting and economic concepts of income, and suggestions have been made, in relation to each model, for segregating 'real' from inflationary value changes. This can be done by ensuring that opening capital, once valued either in historic, contemporary or future terms, be measured in the same general monetary purchasing power terms as closing capital. The problem that then arises, however, is that of selecting an appropriate measure of general purchasing power to apply to capital. Indeed, it may be argued that, at the present time, no such measure exists for this purpose. (The problems of price-level changes will be discussed in greater detail in Chapter 10.)

From these brief comments, it should be clear that the adjustment to stabilize the general purchasing power of the monetary measuring unit is a price-level adjustment over and above any specific price adjustment recognized and measured in the various accounting and economic models. It attempts to segregate that part of the specific price-level adjustment which is an inflationary value change in capital, thereby eliminating it from the resultant income figure.

It should be relatively clear, too, that price-level adjustments, as distinct from measured value changes, result from the use of a measuring unit which has an economic value in terms of its general purchasing power. Because such price-level adjustments involve a restatement of opening capital to ensure comparability of capital in purchasing power terms when determining income, it is also apparent that they are part of the concept and process of capital maintenance – i.e. concerned with maintaining capital in the same generalized purchasing power terms. Such adjustments are not part of the valuation process attributable to capital measurement. Value, therefore, determines capital at the beginning and end of the period concerned, and capital maintenance (incorporating general price-level restatements) determines how much of the resultant value increment is income, and how much of it is simply a restatement of opening capital.[24] As Gynther[25] suggests, in income determination it is value which is the variable and price-level restatement which is the constant, for the latter is capable of being applied to each income model.

As mentioned above, the main problem connected with price-level restatement is one of finding an appropriate measure of generalized monetary purchasing power so as to make the necessary capital maintenance adjustments. There are two main categories of price-level indices reflecting price movements over time: general and specific indices. General indices, normally expressed in terms of average changes in consumer or retail purchasing power, are intended to reflect overall changes in the value of money as a means of exchange, and therefore seem appropriate to the type of capital maintenance adjustment described above. Specific indices, however, reflect particular price changes over time for particular goods and services, and therefore are not directly relevant to segregating income from capital adjustments.

## Summary

The previous sections of this chapter have attempted to outline the separate but related identities of income, capital maintenance and valuation. The relationships can be summarised in the following manner:

**Illustration 1  The income and value function**

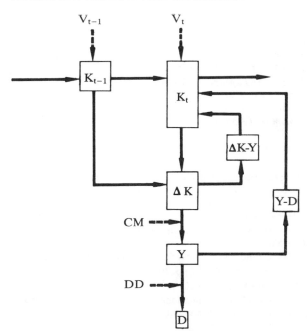

Opening capital $(K_{t-1})$ increases to closing capital $(K_t)$ at t because of valuations $(V)$ made at $t-1$ and t, and thereby results in a capital increment $(\Delta K)$ at t. The problem then is of deciding how much of $\Delta K$ is to be treated as income for the period $(Y)$, and how much has to be retained $(\Delta K - Y)$ in order to maintain opening capital $K_{t-1}$. This is called the process of capital maintenance (CM). In addition, once income Y has been obtained, there is the problem of deciding (DD) how much of Y is required to be consumed or distributed (D) and how much can be retained until the next period $(Y-D)$. The latter process is akin to the dividend decision in business.

### References

(See page 177 for Selected Bibliography)

1. See, for example, W. A. Paton and A. C. Littleton, *An Introduction to Corporate Accounting Standards*, American Accounting Association, 1940, pp. 14–18.

2. I. Fisher, *The Theory of Interest*, Macmillan, 1930, pp. 3–35 (reprinted as 'Income and Capital', in R. H. Parker and G. C. Harcourt (eds.), *Readings in the Concept and Measurement of Income*, Cambridge University Press, 1969, pp. 33–53, esp. p. 46).

3. For example, S. Alexander, 'Income Measurement in a Dynamic Economy', revised by D. Solomons and in W. T. Baxter and S. Davidson (eds.), *Studies in Accounting Theory*, Sweet & Maxwell, 1962, pp. 126–59 amd 174–88.

4. Fisher, *The Theory of Interest*, founded on his basic work, *The Nature of Capital and Income*, Macmillan, 1906.

5. P. H. Wueller, in 'Concepts of Taxable Income: The German Contribution', *Political Science Quarterly*, LIII, 1938, pp. 83–110 (reprinted in Parker and Harcourt (eds.), op. cit., pp. 141–60), in fact describes earlier German efforts to develop the concept.

6. J. R. Hicks, *Value and Capital*, Clarendon Press, 2nd edition, 1946, pp. 171–81 (reprinted as 'Income' in Parker and Harcourt (eds.), op. cit., pp. 74–82).

7. See, for example, N. Kaldor, *An Expenditure Tax*, Allen & Unwin, 1955, pp. 54–78 (reprinted as 'The Concept of Income in Economic Theory' in Parker and Harcourt (eds.), op. cit., pp. 161–82).

8. J. B. Canning, *The Economics of Accountancy: a Critical Analysis of Accounting Theory*, The Ronald Press, 1929, p. 16.

9. Fisher, in Parker and Harcourt (eds.), op. cit., esp. p. 40.

10. ibid.

11. E. Lindahl, 'The Concept of Income', *Economic Essays in Honour of Gustav Cassel*, Allen & Unwin, 1933, pp. 399–407 (reprinted in Parker and Harcourt (eds.), op. cit., pp. 54–62).

12. Hicks, in Parker and Harcourt (eds.), op. cit.

13. K. Boulding, 'Economics and Accounting: the Uncongenial Twins', in Baxter and Davidson (eds.), op. cit., p. 52.

14. Fisher, *The Theory of Interest* and *The Nature of Capital and Income*.

15. Hicks, in Parker and Harcourt (eds.), op cit., pp. 76–8.

16. Lindahl, in Parker and Harcourt (eds.), op. cit., p. 54.

17. Y. Ijiri, 'Physical Measures and Multi-Dimensional Accounting', in R. K. Jaedicke, Y. Ijiri and O. Nielsen (eds.), *Research in Accounting Measurement*, American Accounting Association, 1966, pp. 150–64.

18. R. R. Sterling, *Theory of the Measurement of Enterprise Income*, University of Kansas Press, 1970, p. 28.

19. R. T. Sprouse, 'The Measurement of Financial Position and Income: Purpose and Procedure', in Jaedicke, Ijiri and Nielsen (eds.), op. cit., p. 108.

20. K. MacNeal, *Truth in Accounting*, Scholars Book Co., 1970 (reprint), p. 84.

21. Hicks, in Parker and Harcourt (eds.), op. cit.

22. MacNeal, *Truth in Accounting*, pp. 100–1.

23. Canning, *The Economics of Accounting*, pp. 182–4 and pp. 206–47.

24. See K. Shwayder, 'The Capital Maintenance Rule and the Net Asset Valuation Rule', *Accounting Review*, April 1969, pp. 304–16.

25. R. S. Gynther, 'Capital Maintenance, Price Changes and Profit Determination', *Accounting Review*, October 1970, p. 721.

# 2 The income measurement function

## Purposes and reasons for income measurement

It is only in recent times that accountants have in financial accounting theory and practice concentrated primarily on income. Prior to the late 1920s, the main emphasis in financial reporting was on the balance sheet as a statement of the financial soundness and solvency of a business entity. The reason for this may well have been due to the position of bankers, lenders and creditors as the major external contributors of financial resources to business entities, and hence the main users of any published financial statements. These persons and institutions, being concerned with the immediate and short-term future liquidity of entities, naturally tended to be more interested in the balance sheet than the income statement. The latter report was therefore relegated to a secondary position in financial reporting, being used mainly for establishing the reasonableness of dividend payments. Indeed, it was not until the 1930s and 1940s that the publication of income statements became a regular feature of financial reporting.

However, the gradual development of a sophisticated investment community and market, and the consequent need for accounting information relevant for investor protection and decision making, resulted in the income statement eventually superseding the balance sheet as the primary reporting statement. This has now caused the measurement of accounting income to appear to predominate over the corresponding measurements of assets, liabilities and residual equity.

Income is an important element of the capitalist, free-enterprise economy. It symbolizes wealth accumulation, and characterizes success in such a system: the bigger the income, the larger the assumed success. (Many individuals would, of course, disagree, on social and political grounds, with this crude comparison.) There does indeed exist a significant goal in the free-enterprise economic model – that of income maximization. Such a business objective inevitably provides the need in decision making for accounting measures of income which, according to Canning,[1] are nothing more than indices of business progress and wealth accumulation. Income in this sense therefore represents an incentive in its reported form. It is a measurement of actual business achievement which can be compared with previous hopes, expectations and predictions of performance. It can also be regarded as an indicator of past business activity and behaviour which can be used as a guide to future activity and behaviour. Income therefore has a substantial part to play in influencing human behaviour. As such, it is an operational concept of practical significance: useful and relevant in the field of investment decision making when past and potential business performances are being evaluated.

In contrast to the accountant, the economist's main interest in the micro-economic concept of income is its usefulness as a theoretical tool for analysing the economic behaviour of the individual – i.e. in terms of maximizing his present consumption without impairing his future consumption by eroding his economic capital. (This particular idea is dealt with by Hicks[2] in his concept of 'welloffness' already discussed on pages 7–8.) Economic income is used as a theoretical model to rationalize the economic behaviour of human beings, and so, in consequence, it has strong psychological overtones. In this particular respect it therefore bears some resemblance to accounting income, which measures, in aggregate terms, the results of human activity, and which, through use, modifies and influences human behaviour. In other words, economic income rationalizes on human behaviour, while accounting income measures the results of it.

One further reason for the economist's interest in income is its use as a basis for taxation capacity. It is, as Kaldor[3] has shown, a useful measure which can be taxed to redistribute wealth and economic resources between individuals. Thus business entities are taxed on profits derived from their operational activities, and the basic rules for computing these profits are prescribed by government by means of fiscal legislation.

The economist therefore has significant reasons for recognizing and analysing micro-economic income, but they are far less varied than those of the accountant, who measures it mainly for reporting and decision-making purposes. The following indicate some of these major decision areas to which measured accounting income information is applied in practice.

**1** Income as a guide to dividend and retention policy – i.e. when management has to determine how much of an entity's periodic wealth increase can be distributed to its owners, and how much should be retained to maintain or expand its activities.

**2** Income as a measure of the effectiveness of an entity's management – i.e. when investors attempt to measure the quality of its policy-making, decision-making and controlling activities.

**3** Income as a means of predicting the future income of an entity for purposes of evaluating the worth of an existing or potential investment in it – i.e. when making investment decisions.

**4** Income as a measure of management's stewardship of an entity's resources – i.e. when reporting income as the operational consequence of utilizing these resources on behalf of ownership.

**5** Income as a means of evaluating the worth of past decisions and of improving future decisions – this can apply to all decision makers connected with an entity; i.e. to business managers as well as to investors, lenders, creditors, etc.

**6** Income as a managerial aid in a variety of decision areas within and outside the entity – for example, when reviewing pricing policy, in collective bargaining procedures, when determining legal rights and obligations, when determining the creditworthiness of an entity, and in governmental social and economic regulation (as with retail prices in a monopoly situation).

These are just a few areas in which accounting income can have a part to play in the planning, decision-making and controlling functions related to a business entity. It is therefore clear that it has a varied and significant role in the economic affairs to which the accountant and the economist bring their respective skills and expertise. This has been very clearly evidenced in several recent studies which have sought improvements in the measurement and reporting of accounting data, generally, and income data, particularly. Studies in the UK,[4] the US,[5] and Australia[6] have each sought to demonstrate the importance of measuring and reporting periodic income (and related capital) in light of the needs of defined report user groups. The specification of these groups and their information needs is not easy, and not really within the remit of this particular text. However, the above list of the uses to which income data can be put is sufficient to reveal that the groups will include entity management, owners and investors, lenders and creditors, employees and trade unions, and government agencies. Their information requirements are varied, but all have one thing in common – they need income data with which to make and monitor decisions. In other words, reported income measurements are generally conceived as being useful for predicting and comparing with future data.

## Criteria for income measurement

It seems obvious to say that the various concepts and measurements of income should meet the needs and requirements of their particular users. The existence of specific criteria with which to judge the suitability, validity and reliability of the various income models should not be in doubt. Surprisingly, however, with the possible exception of Chambers[7] and Sterling,[8] few writers on income determination have specified in detail such necessary criteria. This omission is gradually being rectified in the recent publications of professional and other bodies, but only in the context of providing lists of suitable characteristics of financial reports – e.g., the Trueblood Study Group[9] specified qualitative characteristics such as relevance and materiality, form and substance, reliability, freedom from bias, comparability, consistency and understandability. A very similar list was provided by the Accounting Standards Committee[10] and the Sandilands Committee,[11] emphasizing their relevance to any accounting system rather than to detailed systems of income and capital measurement. This absence of more specific income-orientated criteria from the relevant literature is all the more surprising in accounting, where income information is not only measured but is also communicated and used by identifiable persons and institutions. The present section is intended, albeit briefly, to redress some of this imbalance, and owes much to the previous work of Sterling.[12] It should be noted that, on occasion in later chapters where relevant, use will be made of certain of these criteria. However, as the main purpose of this text is to provide an explanation of alternative income and value models, rather than to comment on which is the most relevant in particular circumstances, the use of such criteria will not be as extensive as could be the case with less neutral texts.

The first criterion is that each income model should have utility – i.e. be capable of being used by its user. This is a common-sense point, but one which, because of its simplicity, has tended to be ignored or minimized by many advocates of specific income models. For example, as will be shown at greater length in later chapters, the economist's concept of income, useful when he is rationalizing in a theoretical sense about the behaviour of individuals, is not suitable as a reportable concept for investors and others interested in the overall operational activity of a particular business entity. Likewise, as later sections will show, income based upon replacement costs is useful when the decision to stay in a particular type of business has been made, but it is far less useful when alternative business activities are being contemplated.

Utility, however, despite its simplicity, still remains a rather vague and imprecise criterion. For this reason, Sterling[13] and others[14] have divided it into two main informational criteria: first, relevance (that the particular income model should bear upon or be usefully associated with the decisions of its specified user(s)); and secondly, verity (that the income model should conform with the economic reality it purports to describe in aggregate terms). In other words, a known user should be able to apply the reported measures from a particular income model to his specific range of decisions, and such information should therefore aid him in making these decisions. At the same time, the information about income should correspond truthfully with the economic activity it portrays. This, again, is important, especially in the practical area of accounting income information, although it is also pertinent to the economist who is concerned with using a theoretical model which corresponds closely to the hypothetical behaviour of the economic man he is studying.

The descriptions of relevance and verity in the previous paragraph lead on to consideration of a related criterion – the entity concept which pertains to the identity of the subject of reporting and the persons to whom it is directed. As such, it is a summary and extension of relevance and verity, and can be divided into two main accounting approaches to income and value measurement – those which concentrate on measures related to the proprietorial interests in the reporting entity, and those which concentrate on general-purpose measures of the entity itself. Unfortunately, as has been demonstrated recently,[15] little attention appears to be paid in practice to this criterion when recommendations on income and value are made.

The remaining criteria mainly concern the accountant rather than the economist as they relate to the measurement and communication aspects of income determination; practical topics with which the economist is not so concerned. The measurement criteria concern validity and feasibility: measures of income should be as reliable as possible without conflicting with known time and cost constraints. As Sterling[16] has pointed out, reliable measures of income can only be obtained if there is an adequate measurement scale, employing generally accepted measurement rules and procedures, including the need to ensure that there is additivity within the data being used (there is little point in aggregating data of different types and pretending that the resultant totals have meaning). This view has also been held by a number of other writers,[17] who have emphasized the need to ensure that these measurements are as objective as possible, being verifiable and supported by adequate evidence; in other words, that there should be a minimization of subjectivity in the measurements so as to maximize their reliability. In addition, the measurement of income should not be undertaken at a cost that outweighs the benefits of the information; nor should the time taken to measure income unnecessarily delay the communication of it. So far as communication criteria are concerned, the reported income measures should be understood by the recipient, adequately disclosed and presented, and received before they become outdated. Failing this, the information will either be useless or too out of date to be of relevance to the decisions of the user. Unfortunately, the evidence to date[18] provides little comfort on this point – the meaning of accounting data usually being poorly understood by user groups such as shareholders.

## Alternative income models

The remainder of the book will be concerned with computational descriptions and analytical discussions of the main income and value models briefly described in the Introduction and Chapter 1. The main objectives of each of these models will be explained fully, as will the degree of their conformity to the above-mentioned criteria. The alternatives to be examined are as given in Illustration 2. Chapters 3 to

**Illustration 2  Alternative income and value models**

| Value models* | PV | HC | RC | NRV | CC |
|---|---|---|---|---|---|
| Income concepts† | | | | | |
|   Money income | $Y_e$ | $Y_a$ | $Y_b$ | $Y_r$ | $Y_{cc}$ |
|   'Real' income | $Y_{'e'}$ | $Y_{'a'}$ | $Y_{'b'}$ | $Y_{'r'}$ | $Y_{'cc'}$ |

\* PV is present value; HC is historic cost; RC is
  replacement cost; NRV is net realizable value; and CC
  is current cost.
† $Y_e$ is economic income; $Y_a$ is accounting income; $Y_b$ is
  business income; $Y_r$ is realizable income; and $Y_{cc}$ is
  current cost income.
  $Y_{'e'}$ $Y_{'a'}$ $Y_{'b'}$ $Y_{'r'}$ and $Y_{'cc'}$ are the above incomes
  adjusted for changes in the value of the monetary
  measuring unit.

*Note:* The above income and value terms and symbols will
be used consistently throughout the remainder of the book.

9 inclusive deal with the income concepts when measured in money terms only. They therefore assume a constancy in the general purchasing power of the monetary measuring unit. Chapter 10, on the other hand, relaxes that assumption, and deals with the so-called 'real' income concepts.

## The transactions basis

Most of the main topics to be covered in subsequent chapters have now been introduced. However, one further point deserves a little more comment: the business transactions which underlie the market price based income models.

It was mentioned earlier (page 6) that traditional accounting income is computed in terms of a matching of related operational revenues and costs. These revenues and costs are derived mainly from recorded business transactions, although they are also subject to the specific application of accounting principles such as those involved in depreciation and inventory accounting. Traditional accounting income is therefore firmly based upon recorded transactions which may be evidenced and verified. The same can be said of income models based upon current values, for these utilize the historic cost transactions base before updating the data concerned into contemporary value terms. Therefore, all the income models of the accountant can be said to be soundly based upon past transactions which may be evidenced as having taken place. Differing values (either past or current) may then be applied to the underlying data. In a somewhat less direct way, the various economic income models rely on past transactions – i.e. as justification for the prediction of future flows stemming from the resources which were the subject of past transactions. Transactions are therefore relevant to both the accountant and the economist, if for somewhat different reasons. Thus, the main difference between the two approaches to income is essentially the question of value; the accountant using market prices, and the economist using predictions.

## References

(See page 177 for Selected Bibliography)
1. J. B. Canning, *The Economics of Accountancy*, The Ronald Press, 1929, p. 125.
2. J. R. Hicks, *Value and Capital*, Clarendon Press, 1946, pp. 171–81, reprinted as 'Income', in R. H. Parker and G. C. Harcourt (eds.), *Readings in the Concept and Measurement of Income*, Cambridge University Press, 1969, pp. 74–82.

3. N. Kaldor, *An Expenditure Tax*, Allen & Unwin, 1955, pp. 54–78 (reprinted in Parker and Harcourt (eds.), op. cit., pp. 161–82).

4. Accounting Standards Committee, *The Corporate Report*, 1975; and 'Inflation Accounting', *Report of the Inflation Accounting Committee*, Cmnd 6225, HMSO, 1975.

5. 'Objectives of Financial Statements', *Report of the Study Group on the Objectives of Financial Statements*, American Institute of Certified Public Accountants, 1973.

6. J. W. Kenley and G. J. Staubus, 'Objectives and Concepts of Financial Statements', *Accounting Research Study 3*, Accountancy Research Foundation, 1972.

7. R. J. Chambers, *Accounting, Evaluation and Economic Behaviour*, Prentice-Hall, 1966.

8. R. R. Sterling, *Theory of the Measurement of Enterprise Income*, University of Kansas Press, 1970.

9. *Report of the Study Group on Objectives of Financial Statements*, pp. 57–60.

10. *The Corporate Report*, pp. 28–31.

11. *Report of the Inflation Accounting Committee*, pp. 62–6.

12. Sterling, *Theory of the Measurement of Enterprise Income*, pp. 39–115.

13. ibid., pp. 40–8.

14. For example, T. A. Lee, 'Utility and Relevance – the search for reliable financial accounting information', *Accounting and Business Research*, Summer 1971, pp. 242–9.

15. T. A. Lee, 'The Accounting Entity Concept, Accounting Standards and Inflation Accounting', *Accounting and Business Research*, Spring 1980, pp. 1–11.

16. Sterling, *Theory of the Measurement of Enterprise Income*, pp. 65–115.

17. For example, E. S. Hendriksen, *Accounting Theory*, Irwin, 1977 (3rd edition), pp. 125–34.

18. For example, T. A. Lee and D. P. Tweedie, *The Private Shareholder and the Corporate Report*, Institute of Chartered Accountants in England and Wales, 1977.

# 3 Economic concepts of income and value

## Economic income as consumption

Fisher[1] advocated the restriction of economic income to actual personal consumption because he regarded it as the psychic enjoyment to be derived from consuming goods and services. He treated increases in personal capital (saving) as potential rather than actual consumption – in other words, that saving should not be treated as income until it was consumed and enjoyed. The following example, which will be used and developed throughout this chapter, typifies this approach to income. It should be noted that, for the remainder of the text, the notation $t_0$, $t_1$, $t_2$, ... $t_n$ will be taken to mean point of time $t = 0, 1, 2, ... n$.

> EF purchases 10,000 ordinary shares in AB Ltd at $t_0$ for £11,479. He receives, at annual intervals, the following dividends: at $t_1$ £1,000, at $t_2$ £2,500 and at $t_3$ £3,700. He sells the shares at $t_4$ for £7,000. Assuming EF spent his dividends and sale proceeds on consumer non-durables, then his economic income, according to Fisher, would be: in period $t_0-t_1$ £1,000, in $t_1-t_2$ £2,500, in $t_2-t_3$ £3,700, and in $t_3-t_4$ £7,000; a total of £14,200 which effectively includes returns of capital amounting to his original investment of £11,479. No account is therefore taken of the change in the value of capital during each period.

The factor that matters most in the determination of Fisher's income is whether or not the economic benefits from capital are consumed and enjoyed by the owner of capital. This, of course, is open to severe criticism, mainly on the grounds that capital movements and saving are ignored and, thus, the owner's capital and wellbeing not maintained. In the above example, no account is taken of capital consumption which should have been reinvested in order to maintain EF's future income and wellbeing. (Of the total receipts of £14,200, £11,479 should have been reinvested in order to maintain the flow of future dividends.)

Thus, the Fisher model, because of its psychological basis, ignores economic reality and the need to maintain capital and preserve the wellbeing and future income of the individual. This concept may be useful and relevant when attempting to measure the psychic enjoyment of economic man, but it is less than perfect when attempting to measure the maintenance of his economic wellbeing.

## Economic income as consumption plus saving

Because economists are more interested in analysing the economic behaviour of individuals rather than their psychic experiences, it is not surprising that the generally accepted model for economic income incorporates a measure of the change in economic capital as well as a measure of consumption. Hence their use of the identity mentioned in Chapter 1, $Y_e = C + (K_t - K_{t-1})$; where $Y_e$ is economic income, C is the realised cash flow, $K_t$ is closing capital, and $K_{t-1}$ is opening capital. This model recognizes changes in economic wealth and the need to maintain closing capital at a prescribed opening level before recognizing income. This follows the pattern prescribed by Hicks[2] in his concept of 'welloffness'.

**Illustration 3  Economic income: the Hicks model**

| Period | C £ | $K_t$ £ | $K_{t-1}$ £ | $Y_e$ £ |
|--------|-----|---------|-------------|---------|
| $t_0-t_1$ | 1,000 | 11,282 | 11,479 | 803 |
| $t_1-t_2$ | 2,500 | 9,572 | 11,282 | 790 |
| $t_2-t_3$ | 3,700 | 6,542 | 9,572 | 670 |
| $t_3-t_4$ | 7,000 | — | 6,542 | 458 |
| | 14,200 | | | 2,721 |

Taking the figures given in the previous section and assuming the economic value of the investment to be £11,282 at $t_1$, £9,572 at $t_2$, £6,542 at $t_3$ and (after the sale) £0 at $t_4$, the figures in Illustration 3 would represent economic income in conformity with the previously defined identity $Y_e = C + (K_t - K_{t-1})$. This gives a total economic income of £2,721 for the period $t_0-t_4$, and reveals that, out of the total benefits of £14,200 received for that period, £11,479 (the original capital) should not have been consumed but should, instead, have been reinvested as follows: £197 in period $t_0-t_1$ (£1,000−803), £1,710 in period $t_1-t_2$ (£2,500−790), £3,030 in period $t_2-t_3$ (£3,700−670), and £6,542 in period $t_3-t_4$ (£7,000−458). Thus, if the periodic change in economic capital K is not recognized in the determination of income, there is a danger of overconsumption, lack of capital maintenance and insufficient reinvestment to ensure the flow of future cash for future consumption.

One further question is pertinent to this section before proceeding, and that is of how economic capital is valued. The basis of this measurement is the anticipated flow of cash to be derived from the capital source. As we saw in Chapter 1 (page 9), the economist, by predicting what these future flows might be, computes their present value using fundamental discounting principles.

**Illustration 4  Computation of economic capital K**

| Time | Anticipated flows discounted from | | | | Capital |
|---|---|---|---|---|---|
| | $t_1$ | $t_2$ | $t_3$ | $t_4$ | £ |
| $t_0$ | $\dfrac{£1{,}000}{1\cdot07}$ + | $\dfrac{£2{,}500}{1\cdot07^2}$ + | $\dfrac{£3{,}700}{1\cdot07^3}$ + | $\dfrac{£7{,}000}{1\cdot07^4}$ | = 11,479 |
| $t_1$ | | $\dfrac{£2{,}500}{1\cdot07}$ + | $\dfrac{£3{,}700}{1\cdot07^2}$ + | $\dfrac{£7{,}000}{1\cdot07^3}$ | = 11,282 |
| $t_2$ | | | $\dfrac{£3{,}700}{1\cdot07}$ + | $\dfrac{£7{,}000}{1\cdot07^2}$ | = 9,572 |
| $t_3$ | | | | $\dfrac{£7{,}000}{1\cdot07}$ | = 6,542 |

Using the dividend and sales proceeds from the earlier examples, the figures in Illustration 4 represent the relevant computations of the present value of economic capital at each point in time. The calculations assume a discount rate of 7 per cent, which represents the investor's time-preference rate at which he would be willing to invest a sum of money at the present time. Thus, as each cash flow approaches its point of realization, its present value increases until the realization value is obtained. It then ceases to be part of the existing 'stock' of capital and, instead, represents a realized cash flow which, according to the Hicksian model, is partly income and partly a return of capital requiring reinvestment if capital is to be maintained.

This discounting procedure therefore involves three distinct stages:

(a) identifying the source of potential cash flows (in the above example, 10,000 ordinary shares in AB Ltd); (b) predicting the cash which will be derived from this source over its useful 'lifetime' (in the above example, the annual dividends and the eventual sale proceeds); and (c) applying a discount rate which approximates to the return the individual might obtain if the source invested in was in the best alternative form (for example, if the money was invested in other shares, a building society, or a bank). The practical problems in stages (b) and (c) are significant, however, for there is no such thing as a world of certainty in which future cash flows can be predicted reliably, and where the opportunity cost discount rate can be determined without difficulty and a great deal of subjectiveness. This possibly explains why the economic income model is the most perfect of all models theoretically (in the sense that the value of an individual's capital is related unquestionably to the cash flow which he can expect to derive from it) while being the least perfect practically (in the sense that the value of capital is based upon predictions of events, and therefore upon unverifiable subjective judgements).

The practical imperfections of the economic income model are well known and the theory is subdivided into two main parts: first, an analysis under conditions of certainty; and secondly, a corresponding analysis under conditions of uncertainty. The following sections examine both in greater detail.

## Ideal income

Economic income, measured under conditions of certainty, is usually termed ideal income. In this context, 'certainty' assumes perfect knowledge of the future, in which expectations will be exactly realized and where there will be a perfect market situation in which a constant interest rate operates and is applicable to everyone. It is this utopian situation, first explored by Fisher,[3] which has been assumed in the earlier examples: the predicted annual cash flows of £1,000, £2,500, £3,700 and £7,000 were fully realized, and a constant, unchanging 7 per cent interest rate was applied. Illustration 5 summarizes this situation, following the familiar notation of $Y_e = C + (K_t - K_{t-1})$.

The figures in the illustration show how income, in this situation, is equivalent to interest – i.e. economic income can be derived by taking the given interest rate and applying it to the opening capital of each period. (In $t_0 - t_1$, 7 per cent of £11,479 = £803; in $t_1 - t_2$, 7 per cent of £11,282 = £790; in $t_2 - t_3$, 7 per cent of £9,572 = £670; and in $t_3 - t_4$, 7 per cent of £6,542 = £458.) But this does not show how 'welloffness'

**Illustration 5  Economic income under certainty**

| Period | C<br>£ | $K_t$<br>£ | $K_{t-1}$<br>£ | $Y_e$<br>£ | C−$Y_e$*<br>£ |
|--------|--------|--------|----------|--------|------------|
| $t_0-t_1$ | 1,000 | 11,282 | 11,479 | 803 | 197 |
| $t_1-t_2$ | 2,500 | 9,572 | 11,282 | 790 | 1,710 |
| $t_2-t_3$ | 3,700 | 6,542 | 9,572 | 670 | 3,030 |
| $t_3-t_4$ | 7,000 | — | 6,542 | 458 | 6,542 |
| | 14,200 | | | 2,721 | 11,479 |

* C−$Y_e$ is the periodic return of capital requiring reinvestment.

and future income is to be maintained according to the Hicksian definition given in Chapter 1.

The answer to the problem is reinvestment of that part of the realized cash flows which can be identified as returns of capital. For example, taking the relevant figures from Illustration 3, £197 would be reinvested at 7 per cent at $t_1$ to yield £13 by $t_2$; £1,907 (£197+1,710) would be reinvested at 7 per cent at $t_2$ to yield £133 by $t_3$; £4,937 (£1,907+3,030) would be reinvested at 7 per cent at $t_3$ to yield £345 by $t_4$; and £11,479 (£4,937+6,542) would be reinvested at 7 per cent at $t_4$ to yield £803 indefinitely, so long as the entire capital sum of £11,479 was reinvested annually at 7 per cent.

**Illustration 6  Reinvestment under certainty**

| Period | Economic income from original investment<br>£ | Economic income from reinvestment<br>£ | Total economic income<br>£ |
|--------|-----------------|-----------------|-----------------|
| $t_0-t_1$ | 803 | — | 803 |
| $t_1-t_2$ | 790 | 13 | 803 |
| $t_2-t_3$ | 670 | 133 | 803 |
| $t_3-t_4$ | 458 | 345 | 803 |
| $t_4-t_5$ | — | 803 | 803 |

This is summarized in Illustration 6. In a situation of complete certainty, with expectations accurately predicted and no variation in the interest rate, economic income is identified as interest $K_0$ i; where $K_0$ is the present value of the original capital invested and i is the constant interest rate. However, in order to maintain this level of income (which may be fully consumed without impairing 'welloffness'), capital must be maintained by reinvestment of an appropriate part of the realized stream of cash at each point of realization.

## Income *ex ante*

The perfect world analysed by Fisher is a useful starting point in any examination of economic income. Beyond this, however, it is of limited use because of its lack of practicality in view of the impossibility of predicting the future with certainty. For this reason, the economic income model is normally expressed in terms of a world of uncertainty – a situation corresponding with practical reality. It is a model which follows a similar valuation and computation to that described for ideal income, the only major variation being the recognition of changes in prior expectations of cash, or of changes in the rate of interest used as the discount factor.

As was mentioned in the section on the concept of value in Chapter 1, there are two distinct income models typifying conditions of uncertainty: (a) income *ex ante*, measured at the beginning of the period to which it relates; and (b) income *ex post*, measured at the end of the relevant period. Despite the seemingly historical nature of the latter, both concepts use values which are based upon predictions.

The *ex ante* model reflects Hicks's 'guide to prudent conduct', for it measures the expected income of the period as a proportion of the anticipated realisations for the same period. In other words, it can be identified as $Y_e = C' + (K'_t - K_{t-1})$; where $C'$ is the expected realised cash flow for the period $t-1$ to t, anticipated at $t-1$; $K'_t$ is the closing capital at t, but measured at $t-1$; and $K_{t-1}$ is the opening capital at $t-1$, and measured at that point of time. Income is therefore measured 'before the event' so that the individual to whom it relates has some idea of how much he can consume during the coming period, and of how much he should reinvest of the cash flows he anticipates he will receive during the same period. All figures are based on predictions of cash flows, and consequently there are 'windfall' gains which can occur in this measurement system when prior expectations change in light of new circumstances, or when realized cash flows are different from corresponding predictions. The following example, which makes use of the figures given in previous illustrations as well as the notation mentioned above, describes the computation of income *ex ante*, and

## Illustration 7 Economic income ex ante

| Period | $C'$ £ | $K'_t$ £ | $K_{t-1}$ £ | $Y_e$* £ | $W$† £ | $Y_e+W$‡ £ | $C'-(Y_e+W)$§ £ |
|---|---|---|---|---|---|---|---|
| $t_0-t_1$ | 1,000 | 11,282[(b)] | 11,479[(a)] | 803 | — | 803 | 197 |
| $t_1-t_2$ | 2,500 | 9,572[(c)] | 11,282 | 790 | — | 790 | 1,710 |
| $t_2-t_3$ | 3,700 | 7,477[(e)] | 10,445[(d)] | 732 | 873[(f)] | 1,605 | 2,095 |
| $t_3-t_4$ | 8,000 | — | 7,477 | 523 | — | 523 | 7,477 |
| | 15,200[0] | | | 2,848 | 873 | 3,721[0] | 11,479 |

* Income *ex ante*, after adjusting for changes in expectations of future cash flows.
† Unrealized 'windfall' gain arising from changes in expectations of future cash flows.
‡ Total income *ex ante* inclusive of unrealized 'windfall' gains.
§ Reinvestment necessary to maintain future income and the original capital of £11,479.
[0] Excluding the realized 'windfall' gain of £500 during period $t_3-t_4$; total income *ex ante* inclusive of both realized and unrealized 'windfall' gains would therefore be £3,721 + 500 = £4,221.

(a) $\dfrac{£1,000}{1 \cdot 07} + \dfrac{£2,500}{1 \cdot 07^2} + \dfrac{£3,700}{1 \cdot 07^3} + \dfrac{£7,000}{1 \cdot 07^4}$

(b) $\dfrac{£2,500}{1 \cdot 07} + \dfrac{£3,700}{1 \cdot 07^2} + \dfrac{£7,000}{1 \cdot 07^3}$

(c) $\dfrac{£3,700}{1 \cdot 07} + \dfrac{£7,000}{1 \cdot 07^2}$

(d) $\dfrac{£3,700}{1 \cdot 07} + \dfrac{£8,000}{1 \cdot 07^2}$

(e) $\dfrac{£8,000}{1 \cdot 07}$

(f) $\left[\dfrac{£3,700}{1 \cdot 07} + \dfrac{£8,000}{1 \cdot 07^2}\right] - \left[\dfrac{£3,700}{1 \cdot 07} + \dfrac{£7,000}{1 \cdot 07^2}\right] = £10,445 - 9,572$

also the attendant problems when predictions change or do not equate with realizations.

EF invests in 10,000 shares in AB Ltd at $t_0$ for £11,479. He anticipates, at $t_0$, receipt of dividends of £1,000 at $t_1$, £2,500 at $t_2$ and £3,700 at $t_3$. He also anticipates, at $t_0$, selling the shares for £7,000 at $t_4$. Assume a constant 7 per cent rate of interest, and annual intervals. In addition, assume that EF's original sales proceeds prediction of £7,000 changes to £8,000 at $t_2$; that he then realizes £8,500 at $t_4$; and that his other predictions are all realized in full.

As is shown in note (a) to Illustration 7 (opposite), the original investment cost has been assumed to be equal to the present value of the future cash flows anticipated at $t_0$. This has been done for the sake of simplicity, although the problem of circumstances where the two figures do not equate with one another will be discussed in a later section.

Income *ex ante* is thus the anticipated income of a defined period. As Hicks's 'guide to prudent conduct', it represents the maximum amount the owner of capital anticipates he can consume during the period without impairing his capital and future consumption. The figures in the illustration demonstrate this, and highlight in particular the requirement in this model to adjust opening capital ($K_{t-1}$) whenever there is either a change in expectations or a difference between realization and prediction. These adjustments result in realized and unrealized 'windfall' gains or losses.

'Windfalls', as previously indicated, are capital value increments or decrements which arise when prior expectations of future cash flows are found or believed to be at variance with the cash flows actually received or the expectations currently held. The term 'windfall', attributable to Keynes, is used to denote the unexpected nature of such changes in capital value. The unrealized 'windfall' gain of £873 in this example arises at $t_2$ because EF's expectation of the sale proceeds of his shares at $t_4$ changes from £7,000 to £8,000. This change in the anticipated future cash flows to be derived from his shares (amounting to £1,000 at the time of sale $t_4$) has a value at $t_2$ of £873 if it is discounted appropriately over two years at the assumed 7 per cent interest rate:

i.e. $\dfrac{£1,000}{1 \cdot 07^2} = £873.$

In contrast, the realized 'windfall' gain of £500 arises at $t_4$ when £8,500 is received on the sale of the shares, as compared with the figure of £8,000 which, at $t_3$, had been expected.

In each of the economic income models, assuming constant money values, at least a sum equivalent to the original capital figure should be reinvested gradually throughout the period of investment in which the anticipated cash flows are realized. Thus, in the above example, £11,479 should be accumulated and reinvested in order to comply with the concept of capital maintenance. Any changes in the value of capital due to 'windfall' gains or losses could therefore result in too much or too little reinvestment for capital maintenance purposes. In this case, the 'windfalls' have been added to the computed *ex ante* income on the assumption that the owner of capital wishes to maintain rather than expand it. However, it should also be noted that 'windfall' gains or losses can be treated legitimately as capital readjustments, eventually leading to equivalent reinvestment on realization of the cash flows, if the investment policy is maintenance, not of the original project capital, but of the revised capital at the beginning of each period. Indeed, this would appear to be compatible with the views of Hicks[4] in the sense that such a policy would maintain the present level of income in the future. It would also appear to be relevant to the situation of a continuing business wishing to maintain an expanding (or contracting) capital. However, there are no easy solutions to this problem and, in order to avoid confusing the reader with the need to maintain a fluctuating capital figure, the remainder of this chapter will assume a maintenance of the original project investment.

It should also be noted that 'windfall' gains or losses may not be as easily identified as either capital or income. For example, the original investment cost may not be fully determinable, as in the case of a person investing his own skills and experience, and which he does not therefore need to purchase. It is thus difficult to establish the value of capital to be maintained or whether future purchasing will need to be undertaken to replace such 'free' capital. In these circumstances, the original investment could be valued as the sum of the suitably discounted future cash flows, and the difference between this and the total of any sums actually expended on resources underlying capital could be regarded as a form of subjective goodwill. This 'windfall' element arising at the point of original investment could then be treated either as income, if the owner felt it did not require to be maintained by reinvestment, or as capital, if the opposite was the case. Much would therefore depend on the circumstances, and what capital was deemed necessary to maintain. Indeed, there may well be circumstances where 'windfall' gains or losses could be treated partly as income and partly as capital adjustments, as in the situation of resources which originally were 'free' but which will eventually need to be partly replaced by purchase. Whatever is done, much care must be exercised with 'windfall' elements in the economic models to ensure that the appropriate classification has been made to maintain capital and, thus, future income.

Summarizing on the above example, it can therefore be seen that, in total, £15,700 was received during the period $t_0-t_4$, of which £4,221 (original *ex ante* income of £2,848 plus 'windfall' income of £873 and £500) is income, and £11,479 is capital requiring reinvestment in order to maintain future income. It should also be noted, however, that income *ex ante* has as its main goal the computation of an approximate income measure which is an aid to the owner of capital in his consumption and saving activities during an ensuing period. 'Windfall' adjustments must, if at all possible, be made *ex ante* if that aim is to be achieved. This may be done with unrealized 'windfalls' resulting from changes in expectations. But, with realized 'windfalls', the adjustment is *ex post*. Therefore, although it should be made in order to ensure prudent economic behaviour, it does not affect the computation or use of subsequent *ex ante* measures of income. It should also be noted that 'windfall' adjustments can be negative (i.e. representing losses); and that they can also be caused by changes in the personal subjective interest rate used as a discount factor. The adjusting computations nevertheless follow the pattern described in Illustration 7. Finally, as with the ideal income model, the aim of the *ex ante* model is to provide a constant rate of return on capital (in this case 7%) which leaves the recovery of capital (so-called economic depreciation) as the major variable to be dealt with.

## Income *ex post*

The alternative economic income model, based on a world of uncertainty, produces income *ex post* – i.e. income which is measured at the end rather than the beginning of each relevant period. As with income *ex ante*, it requires predictions of cash flows to value opening and closing capital; and it also incorporates adjustments for realized and unrealized 'windfall' gains. Unlike the *ex ante* model, however, these adjustments can be made to past as well as to future capital values. Illustration 8, using the same figures and assumptions as for income *ex ante*, describes the computation of income *ex post*. This, it will be remembered, is identified as $Y_e = C + (K_t - K'_{t-1})$; where C is the actual realised cash flow of the period; $K_t$ is the closing capital measured at

## Illustration 8 Economic income ex post

| Period | C £ | $K_n$ £ | $K'_{n-1}$ £ | $Y_e^*$ £ | W† £ | $Y_e+W$‡ £ | $C-(Y_e+W)$§ £ |
|---|---|---|---|---|---|---|---|
| $t_0-t_1$ | 1,000 | 11,282[b] | 11,479[a] | 803 | — | 803 | 197 |
| $t_1-t_2$ | 2,500 | 10,445[d] | 12,098[c] | 847 | 816[e] | 1,663 | 837 |
| $t_2-t_3$ | 3,700 | 7,477[f] | 10,445 | 732 | — | 732 | 2,968 |
| $t_3-t_4$ | 8,500 | — | 7,944[g] | 556 | 467[h] | 1,023 | 7,477 |
| | 15,700 | | | 2,938 | 1,283 | 4,221 | 11,479 |

\* Income *ex post*, after adjusting for changes in expectations and realizations of future cash flows.

† 'Windfall' gains due to changes in expectations and eventual realizations of future cash flows.

‡ Total income *ex post*, inclusive of all 'windfall' gains.

§ Reinvestment necessary to maintain future income and the original capital of £11,479.

(a) $\dfrac{£1,000}{1\cdot07} + \dfrac{£2,500}{1\cdot07^2} + \dfrac{£3,700}{1\cdot07^3} + \dfrac{£7,000}{1\cdot07^4}$

(b) $\dfrac{£2,500}{1\cdot07} + \dfrac{£3,700}{1\cdot07^2} + \dfrac{£7,000}{1\cdot07^3}$

(c) $\dfrac{£2,500}{1\cdot07} + \dfrac{£3,700}{1\cdot07^2} + \dfrac{£8,000}{1\cdot07^3}$

(d) $\dfrac{£3,700}{1\cdot07} + \dfrac{£8,000}{1\cdot07^2}$

(e) £12,098 − 11,282

(f) $\dfrac{£8,000}{1\cdot07}$

(g) $\dfrac{£8,500}{1\cdot07}$

(h) £7,944 − 7,477

the end of the period; and $K'_{t-1}$ is the opening capital, again measured at the end of the period, and therefore including any revisions due to changes in expectations or realizations.

The readjustment of opening capital, resulting in 'windfall' gains, follows a similar computational pattern to that described for income *ex ante*. However, so far as the *ex post* 'windfall' gains are concerned (£816 and £467 in Illustration 8) their treatment as income elements is, in this example, entirely similar to the *ex ante* model approach. Not to treat them as income would result in the over-recovery of capital for reinvestment and the maintenance of future income at levels higher than that conceived from the original investment (a policy, as mentioned previously, incompatible with Hicksian thought). The previously mentioned problems of the partial treatment of 'windfalls' as income in circumstances when the original investment cost is indeterminate, or their treatment entirely as capital, would apply to the *ex post* model in the same way as in the *ex ante* model.

Finally, it ought to be noted that the *ex post* model described in this section is not entirely reliant on ex post events. In fact, it is similar to the *ex ante* model in its reliance on forecasts of realised cash flows. Consequently, it uses past and future flows to determine income – a situation akin to the measurement of periodic income by the accountant.

## A comparative analysis

It is now appropriate to compare separately the three concepts of economic income so far discussed: ideal income, income *ex ante* and income *ex post*. From such a comparison, the main problems, similarities and dissimilarities may be summarized. Use will be made of earlier examples, then looked at in greater detail.

Assuming the situation and data used in the computation of income *ex ante* and income *ex post*, it is possible to compute ideal income – i.e. income measured completely *ex post* at point $t_4$. By so doing, the problem of changes in expectations and realizations is avoided. 'Windfall' gains resulting from these changes are also avoided. This does not mean, however, that 'windfalls' cannot appear in the ideal model. They do arise at the point of original investment when the actual investment cost is different from the computed present value of anticipated cash flows. Illustration 9 contains such a 'windfall' gain. The problem here, as with other occasions involving 'windfall' elements, is whether the gain (or loss) is income, capital or a mixture of both.

In this example, EF should have reinvested £11,479 at 7 per cent by

## Illustration 9 Ideal economic income ex post

| Period | C £ | $K_t$ £ | $K_{t-1}$ £ | $Y_e$* £ | W† £ | $Y_e+W$‡ £ | $C-(Y_e+W)$§ £ |
|---|---|---|---|---|---|---|---|
| $t_0-t_1$ | 1,000 | 12,507[b] | 12,623[a] | 884 | 1,144[c] | 2,028 | (1,028) |
| $t_1-t_2$ | 2,500 | 10,882[d] | 12,507 | 875 | — | 875 | 1,625 |
| $t_2-t_3$ | 3,700 | 7,944[e] | 10,882 | 762 | — | 762 | 2,938 |
| $t_3-t_4$ | 8,500 | — | 7,944 | 556 | — | 556 | 7,944 |
| | 15,700 | | | 3,077 | 1,144 | 4,221 | 11,479 |

\* Ideal income *ex post*, after adjusting for the change in opening capital.
† The 'windfall' gain due to the original investment cost being exceeded by the original economic value of the investment.
‡ Ideal income *ex post*, including the opening 'windfall' gain.
§ Reinvestment required to maintain future income and the original capital of £11,479.

(a) $\dfrac{£1,000}{1\cdot07} + \dfrac{£2,500}{1\cdot07^2} + \dfrac{£3,700}{1\cdot07^3} + \dfrac{£8,500}{1\cdot07^4}$

(b) $\dfrac{£2,500}{1\cdot07} + \dfrac{£3,700}{1\cdot07^2} + \dfrac{£8,500}{1\cdot07^3}$

(c) £12,623 − 11,479

(d) $\dfrac{£3,700}{1\cdot07} + \dfrac{£8,500}{1\cdot07^2}$

(e) $\dfrac{£8,500}{1\cdot07}$

$t_4$, leaving the remaining £4,221 available for consumption, including the opening 'windfall' gain of £1,144. These figures correspond, of course, with income *ex ante* and *ex post* after adjustment for 'windfall' gains, and assume that the latter are entirely of an income nature, as previously assumed. Illustrations 10 and 11 gather together all the relevant figures from the three models for comparative purposes. The figures in these illustrations highlight the points of interest which are listed overleaf.

**Illustration 10 Comparative summary of economic incomes**

| Period | Ideal income | | Income *ex ante* | | Income *ex post* | |
|---|---|---|---|---|---|---|
| | (1) £ | (2) £ | (1) £ | (2) £ | (1) £ | (2) £ |
| $t_0-t_1$ | 884 | 2,028 | 803 | 803 | 803 | 803 |
| $t_1-t_2$ | 875 | 875 | 790 | 790 | 847 | 1,663 |
| $t_2-t_3$ | 762 | 762 | 732 | 1,605 | 732 | 732 |
| $t_3-t_4$ | 556 | 556 | 523 | 1,023 | 556 | 1,023 |
| | 3,077 | 4,221 | 2,848 | 4,221 | 2,938 | 4,221 |

(1) = before inclusion of 'windfall' gains.
(2) = after inclusion of 'windfall' gains.

**Illustration 11 Comparative summary of reinvestment**

| Period | Ideal income £ | Income *ex ante* £ | Income *ex post* £ |
|---|---|---|---|
| $t_0-t_1$ | (1,028) | 197 | 197 |
| $t_1-t_2$ | 1,625 | 1,710 | 837 |
| $t_2-t_3$ | 2,938 | 2,095 | 2,968 |
| $t_3-t_4$ | 7,944 | 7,477 | 7,477 |
| | 11,479 | 11,479 | 11,479 |

(a) With all the facts known; total income for the period $t_0-t_4$ amounts to £4,221, being total receipts of £15,700 minus the original capital investment of £11,479. This is ideal income *ex post* and identifies with the total traditional accounting income that would have been derived from these figures.

(b) If the 'welloffness' of EF, represented by the actual cost of £11,479 of his investment at $t_0$, is to be maintained, then £11,479 must be available for reinvestment by $t_4$ in order to provide an annual 7 per cent return on capital of £803 indefinitely (assuming there was no future change in the interest rate).

(c) Both income *ex ante* and income *ex post* are based on expectations which can change over time, thereby affecting income and capital value computations. Both therefore require an acknowledgement of the existence of 'windfall' gains or losses, and a consideration of whether each such 'windfall' is entirely of an income or capital nature, or whether it is partly a capital adjustment and partly income due to the indeterminate value of the original investment cost or future replacement policy. Owing to the 'windfall' adjustments, neither the *ex ante* nor *ex post* models can be said to be accurate substitutes for the ideal model with its advantage of certainty. Thus they are advocated only as *guides* to prudent economic behaviour: extremely useful for decisions, but of little advantage for stewardship.

(d) Income *ex ante* and income *ex post* are both better guides to future economic behaviour than ideal income *ex post*. The latter model is completely irrelevant as such a guide because it can only be computed after the investment has been terminated. It is intended to fulfil a stewardship or accountability function, whereas the uncertainty models are intended for decision functions.

(e) 'Windfall' gains resulting from changing expectations and realizations are to be found in both the uncertainty income models and the ideal model. If they are treated solely as capital adjustments, the emphasis is on maintaining the revised opening capital of each period. If, on the other hand, they are treated solely as income, there are the dangers, in certain well-defined circumstances where the original investment cost or future resource replacements are indeterminate, of over-consumption, insufficient reinvestment, and a lack of maintenance of 'welloffness'.

### Underlying assumptions of economic income

The various economic models of income and value appear, at first sight, to be extremely useful. They attempt to value all resources (human and otherwise) underlying capital; they provide measures of consumption necessary to maintain an individual's economic well-being, and thus to regulate his consumption behaviour; they value on the basis of predictions, this being particularly relevant in the area of economic decision making; their valuation processes take into account the important factor of timing (potential economic benefits becoming more valuable as the relevant realization dates are approached), and returns of capital are specified as guides to reinvestment and capital maintenance; and they are expressed as entirely personal concepts, which makes their subjective nature tolerable.

However, the economic model contains certain fundamental assumptions which are open to criticism, mainly from the point of view of practicality. The first one concerns the need to predict future cash flows. Forecasting in a world of certainty would be an effortless process because the future could be anticipated with perfect foresight. Unfortunately, no such world exists in reality, and the predicted cash flows upon which incomes *ex ante* and *ex post* depend are subject to a great deal of uncertainty. This, in turn, leads to 'windfall' gains and losses which have to be treated with great care if reinvestment is to be conducted adequately. In practice, the use of the economic income model would therefore founder on the extreme subjectiveness and inaccuracies of the required predictions – the accuracy of the income measure as a guide to prudent conduct being significantly dependent on the accuracy of the underlying forecasts.

A second problem arises in connection with the choice of the discount factor used in computing the present value of opening and closing economic capital. Rates of interest vary according to the relevant investment, as well as over time. The choice of rate depends on the individual's preferences and the availability of alternative investments. Such choice and variation leads inevitably to an increase in the subjectiveness of the resultant income measure: different discount factors produce entirely different measures of income. Such potential variation renders doubtful the practicality of using economic income as an operational measure to guide decision makers.

A third problem affecting the economic income model concerns the timing of the realization of cash flows whose aggregate present value constitutes a measure of economic capital. In other words, the forecasting problem mentioned above does not solely concern the prediction of the money value of flows; it also concerns the timing of their receipt of these benefits. Different realization times produce different measures of capital, and thus of income. Inaccuracies in the forecasting of realization dates will therefore produce corresponding inaccuracies in the income measure.

The fourth problem affecting the validity and feasibility of the economic income model arises out of the concept of capital maintenance. The need to maintain opening capital before recognizing income has been explained already – as has the attendant problem of reinvestment. Returns of capital included in the realized cash flow figure must be reinvested at the same interest rate used as a discount factor if capital and future income is to be maintained. Reinvestment of this kind is, however, based on further assumptions – that, for example, reinvestment can be made and that interest rates will remain constant. It also requires predictions (including timing) of cash which will flow from reinvestment. In a world of uncertainty, this will produce inaccuracies, variations and, in consequence, further 'windfalls'. It will also produce another problem: that such reinvestment creates further returns of capital requiring reinvestment; and so on, in the form of a chain reaction with a disappearing time horizon which will increase the subjectiveness of forecasts. Presumably, though, it may be assumed, when looking at an individual's economic income, that his model will have a definite end point corresponding with his date of death. Yet even this will demand subjective forecasting. Thus the 'open-ended' nature of the economic model, caused by the requirement of reinvestment, further emphasizes its highly theoretical structure.

The final problem to be mentioned at this stage is, again, one involving forecasting. So far, the explanations relevant to the economic income model have assumed a static situation: that an individual will attempt to maintain his 'welloffness' at a constant level. In fact, it seems reasonable to assume that individuals will, on the whole, attempt to maximize their 'welloffness' by investing capital in activities which will yield increasing benefits over time. Therefore, in forecasting cash flows for discounting purposes, a significant problem would be the possible element of growth to incorporate, assuming growth of capital to be one of the objectives of the person concerned. The choice of such a growth factor further increases the subjectiveness of the economic model.

## Summary

It therefore seems that the validity and feasibility of the economic income model in a world of uncertainty are severely constrained by the requirement to forecast future cash flows (this also involving the attendant problems of timing of benefits, reinvestment predictions and growth factors); and the choice of an appropriate discount factor dependent on the investment preferences and alternatives open to the individual. For these reasons, the model does not appear to satisfy the main measurement criteria which are generally accepted by accountants – i.e. reliability and objectivity. On the other hand, the model does conform with the general criterion of relevance and, for this reason, should not be dismissed out of hand as having no utility. As a model, it contains most of the ingredients which an individual should be concerned with in regulating his personal economic affairs: value of capital in terms of anticipated benefits, the danger of overconsumption which can impair future wellbeing, and the consequent need to maintain capital and to reinvest. On these grounds, the economic model must continue to remain of use to economic man – not as a reportable concept for decision-making purposes, but as a theoretical model for analysis purposes; a model which helps to identify the significant factors determining an individual's 'welloffness'.

## Economic income as an entity concept

As has been seen, micro-economic income is normally conceived as a personal concept. This is obviously pertinent to the economist who attempts to rationalize, in general terms, the behaviour of individuals, but it is hardly relevant to the accountant, who is concerned mainly with measuring and reporting on the economic affairs and activities of such specific business entities as partnerships, companies, nationalized industries, government departments, and so forth. Therefore, the question arises as to whether or not the personal economic model (as expressed in the basic identity $Y_e = C + (K_t - K_{t-1})$) can be adapted to the business entity.[5] If this were the case, then capital K would represent the present value of anticipated distributions[6] for the life of the entity; and C would represent either the anticipated distributions for the ensuing period (in the *ex ante* model) or the actual distributions for the past period (in the *ex post* model).

Following on the above brief comments, several points can be made. First, all the problems related to the personal economic model are also relevant to the entity model – i.e. forecasting of cash distributions, selection of an appropriate discount factor, timing of distributions, and changes in expectations and realizations causing 'windfalls'. Secondly, apart from the previously mentioned problems, there is the additional problem related to forecasting that the business entity may well have an indefinite life requiring distributions to be predicted for many years ahead. The potential subjectiveness and inherent inaccuracies in this process are obvious; as is the lack of correspondence with the criteria of reliability and objectivity. Thirdly, it is possible to have a computed economic income measure for a period when the entity does not distribute ($K_t$ and $K_{t-1}$ would still require to be computed despite the non-existence of C). And lastly, following from this last point, entity economic income cannot really be said to be representative of managerial activity and performance in a defined period, since it relies to a great extent on anticipated activity, etc., of future rather than past or current periods.

## References

(See page 177 for Selected Bibliography)

1. I. Fisher, *The Theory of Interest*, Macmillan, 1930, pp. 3–35, reprinted as 'Income and Capital', in R. H. Parker and G. C. Harcourt (eds.), *Readings in the Concept and Measurement of Income*, Cambridge University Press, 1969, pp. 33–53.

2. J. R. Hicks, *Value and Capital*, Clarendon Press, 2nd edition, 1946, pp. 171–81, (reprinted as 'Income', in Parker and Harcourt (eds.), op. cit., pp. 74–82).

3. Fisher, *The Theory of Interest*.

4. Hicks, *Value and Capital*, p. 179.

5. See S. Alexander, 'Income Measurement in a Dynamic Economy', revised by D. Solomons, in W. T. Baxter and S. Davidson (eds.), *Studies in Accounting Theory*, Sweet & Maxwell, 1962, pp. 126–200.

6. Cash distributions rather than net cash inflows of the entity have been taken as the basis for this adaptation in order to avoid the problem of double-counting of cash flows due to reinvestment (see M. H. Miller and F. Modigliani, 'Dividend Policy, Growth, and the Valuation of Shares', *Journal of Business*, 1961, pp. 411–33).

# 4 The traditional accounting concept of income

## Nature and purpose of accounting income

The theoretically perfect income model of the economist has been outlined in Chapter 3. Its undoubted failure to satisfy so many of the measurement and communication criteria usually recognized by the practising accountant focuses attention on another income concept which goes beyond the theory stage and is measured and reported widely throughout free enterprise economies. This is the traditional accounting concept of income which uses past business transactions as its foundation. The aim of the present chapter is to explain the nature of this practical concept of income; the main principles and conventions which underlie it; the significant points for and against its use in practice; and to make a comparative analysis with the basic economic model.

The origins of contemporary financial reporting of income are in the history of the development of companies and investment markets in the late nineteenth and early twentieth centuries. Over that period, investment markets were largely undeveloped, most of the finance required to run businesses coming either from owner-managers or from bankers, lenders and creditors. The need for externally reported accounting information was, however, limited to the latter groups. They required a knowledge of company solvency, and consequently the balance sheet rather than the income statement was their primary interest and concern. In those days, as Sterling[1] has pointed out, accountants had the task of curbing the natural enthusiasm of owner-managers in reporting unrealistically optimistic portrayals of company solvency in their balance sheets. This function led, for reporting purposes, to the traditional accounting approach of conservative valuation, and it has remained an integral part of financial reporting to this day. Despite this, in the early days of financial reporting, conservative valuations had little effect on income measurement since income was then practically non-existent as a reporting concept.

Gradually, as business and trade expanded, the need for corporate finance far outstripped the capability of bankers and lenders to provide it, and so the rapid development of capital markets and investment communities was ensured. The introduction in this way of large numbers of external investors created the need for investor protection and the corresponding requirement that management should account periodically for its efforts on behalf of ownership. Thus the significance of income as a measure of managerial performance came gradually to be realized, until, today, it is generally accepted as one of the most significant pieces of information used by investors and others interested in the financial affairs of businesses. During the 1920s and 1930s, the balance sheet slowly ceased to be the primary financial report, becoming instead the residual statement resulting from the process of measuring periodic accounting income. The growing importance of reportable business income was further aided by the increasingly sophisticated and onerous tax system which caused business management to concentrate on the measurement of accounting income figures which could serve as the basis for computing taxation liabilities. The need to ensure that periodic dividend and interest distributions were adequately covered by available income must have similarly focused managements' attentions on income determination.

What this introductory commentary has attempted to show is how the traditional concept of reported accounting income has developed mainly as a consequence of the development of investment over the last hundred years or so, accentuated by the desire of management lawfully to minimize tax payments. A main purpose of reporting income today is to make management accountable for its efforts on behalf of the owners of capital. An equally important aim, derived from the development of an increasingly sophisticated investment community, is the use of income as an aid to investment decision making at a time when investors are trying to assess the benefits to be derived in investing in a particular business (in particular, to show the potential flow of dividends distributable out of future income). Accounting income is also useful as the basis for computing taxes; assessing the financial position and creditworthiness of a particular business; assessing the risks attached to lending to a business; governmental policy making, particularly in industrial regions needing governmental support and aid; and so on. Most of these aims have one common factor: information about income is used in activities which demand predictions and forecasts (for example, in relation to share dividends and values, repayment of loans and credit, and regional development). These activities therefore appear to be far more relevant to the economist's income concept. Yet, the main income concept used in practice is historical in nature, reflecting past business activity and managerial performance. As Canning[2] has put it, the accountant traditionally measures income as it comes 'down-stream' past a defined point (the reporting date), whereas the economist attempts to trace the possible flow of income from that point. This raises a question to be pursued further throughout this chapter: can a historic measure of income conform with the basic criterion of relevance to a user primarily concerned with the future?

## The transactions basis

The basis for measuring traditional accounting income is the transactions which the business entity enters into with third parties in its operational activities. These transactions relate mainly to revenues received from the sale of goods and/or services, and the various costs incurred in achieving these sales. All these transactions will, in some way, involve the eventual receipt or payment of cash, and, if the eventual cash exchange with third parties is not complete at the moment of measuring income, this incompleteness is allowed for (e.g. by accounting for amounts due by debtors for sales on credit, and for amounts due to creditors for purchases on credit). Once these adjustments have been made, the revenues and costs which have been recognized as having arisen during the defined period are then linked or matched in order to derive accounting income. It is this matching process which gives rise to most judgemental problems in accounting. The recorded costs need to be analysed and segregated; those costs which can be realistically attributed to the revenue of the period are matched with it, and those which cannot be matched are carried forward to subsequent periods to be linked with appropriate revenues in the future. The classic accounting problems of carrying forward costs attributable to such long-lived resources as plant and equipment, or to such trading resources as stock and work in progress, are examples of this allocation process in traditional accounting.[3] It gives rise to the 'residue' balance sheet previously mentioned, i.e. a balance sheet which describes unallocated or unmatched past costs as assets of the business.

Summarizing our arguments so far, the traditional accounting process is, first, to define the particular accounting period; secondly, to recognize the revenues of that period; thirdly, to recognize the corresponding period costs; and fourthly, to match those costs relevant to the recognized revenues, carrying forward the residue of unallocated costs for matching with subsequent periodic revenues.

The resultant computations can then be incorporated in the reported income statement and balance sheet. Illustration 12 typifies this process, assuming the following information:

PQ opened a new business at $t_0$ when he purchased a motor van for £1,200 and shop premises for £5,000. His cash transactions, assuming no stock, debtors or creditors because of the nature of trade,

**Illustration 12 Computation of traditional accounting income**

| Income statements | Period | | | | |
|---|---|---|---|---|---|
| | $t_0-t_1$ £ | $t_1-t_2$ £ | $t_2-t_3$ £ | $t_3-t_4$ £ | Total £ |
| Sales | 10,000 | 15,000 | 11,700 | — | 36,700 |
| Less: operating costs | 8,000 | 12,500 | 10,000 | — | 30,500 |
| | 2,000 | 2,500 | 1,700 | — | 6,200 |
| Less: depreciation | 300[a] | 300[a] | 300[a] | 200[b] | 1,100 |
| Operating income | 1,700 | 2,200 | 1,400 | (200) | 5,100 |
| Capital gain | — | — | — | 5,300[c] | 5,300 |
| Accounting income | 1,700 | 2,200 | 1,400 | 5,100 | 10,400[d] |

| Balance sheets | Time | | | | |
|---|---|---|---|---|---|
| | $t_0$ £ | $t_1$ £ | $t_2$ £ | $t_3$ £ | $t_4$ £ |
| Shop | 5,000 | 5,000 | 5,000 | 5,000 | — |
| Van | 1,200 | 900[e] | 600[f] | 300[g] | — |
| Cash | — | 2,000[h] | 4,500[i] | 6,200[j] | —[k] |
| | 6,200 | 7,900 | 10,100 | 11,500 | — |
| Capital | 6,200 | 7,900[l] | 10,100[m] | 11,500[n] | —[o] |

were: in period $t_0-t_1$, sales £10,000 and operating costs £8,000; in period $t_1-t_2$, sales £15,000 and operating costs £12,500; and in period $t_2-t_3$, sales £11,700 and operating costs £10,000. Immediately after $t_3$, PQ ceased business operations, realizing £100 for the van and £10,300 for the shop, and closed the accounting records. At $t_0$, the van had been estimated to have a four-year life with a nil scrap value at the end of that time. Depreciation, therefore, was to be written off evenly throughout the life of the van. It was felt unnecessary to depreciate the shop.

The simple example of accounting income in Illustration 12 contains many of the points common to the traditional model. It is firmly based on the past transactions of a defined period; it requires the recognition of trading revenues realized during that period; it also requires the identification and allocation of appropriate costs of the period to be matched against these revenues (in this case, the operating costs and van depreciation); any unallocated costs are then carried forward for subsequent allocation, being classified in the meantime as assets (in this case, the book values of the shop and van); gains are normally recognized in the periods in which they are realized (in this case, operating gains and the capital gain from the shop sale); and generally, there is a conservative attitude to valuation – assets being expressed normally in historic cost terms with no account being taken of unrealized value changes (as in the case of the shop). In addition, the example

---

(a) $\frac{1}{4} \times$ £1200; depreciation written off on a straight-line basis over an estimated four-year life; (b) £1,200 − 900 − 100; the loss on realization of the van, computed by deducting the aggregate depreciation provided to date, together with the sale proceeds, from the original cost; (c) £10,300 − 5,000; the sale proceeds of the shop minus its original cost, resulting in a so-called capital gain; (d) (£36,700 + 10,300 + 100) − (£1,200 + 5,000 + 30,500); the total income for the period $t_0-t_4$ which is equivalent to the total receipts from operations, plus the sale proceeds of the shop and the van, minus the total payments incurred in connection with each of these three factors; (e) £1,200 − 300; the cost of the van minus depreciation for the period $t_0-t_1$; (f) £900 − 300; the net book value of the van at $t_1$ minus depreciation for the period $t_1-t_2$; (g) £600 − 300; the net book value of the van at $t_2$ minus depreciation for the period $t_2-t_3$; (h) £0 + 2,000; the cash surplus for the period $t_0-t_1$ from business operations; (i) £2,000 + 2,500; the cash balance at $t_1$ plus the cash surplus for the period $t_1-t_2$ from business operations; (j) £4,500 + 1,700; the cash balance at $t_2$ plus the cash surplus for the period $t_2-t_3$ from business operations; (k) £6,200 + 10,300 + 100 − 16,600; the cash balance at $t_3$ plus the sale proceeds of the shop and the van minus the final distribution to the owner; (l) £6,200 + 1,700; opening capital at $t_0$ plus income retained for the period $t_0-t_1$; (m) £7,900 + 2,200; capital at $t_1$ plus income retained for the period $t_1-t_2$; (n) £10,100 + 1,400; capital at $t_2$ plus income retained for the period $t_2-t_3$; (o) £11,500 + 5,100 − 16,600; capital at $t_3$ plus income and gain for the period $t_3-t_4$ minus the final distribution to the owner.

shows how traditional accounting income is expressed as a matching of revenue and expenditure transactions, and resulting in a series of residues for balance sheet purposes. It can also be interpreted as a periodic change in accounting capital when this is expressed as the aggregate of these residues. Accounting income therefore appears to have the benefit of a sound, factual and objective transactions base. Despite this, however, it must be remembered that the validity of its measurement process depends on the soundness of the judgements involved in revenue recognition and cost allocation, and that there is therefore a great deal of flexibility and subjectiveness involved. Because of this, it is important that the reader be aware at least of the main principles and conventions adhered to in the measurement function.

## The primary measurement principles

It has been suggested[4] that, when management is accounting and reporting on the business activities and affairs of an entity, it is essentially conducting a stewardship function; and that ownership is primarily concerned in this respect with a straightforward account of what management has done with the resources entrusted to it. Therefore, it is further argued, management should not be concerned with measuring and reporting individual resource and aggregate entity values, since aggregate valuations should be the concern of owners. This, of course, ignores the fact that the owners must have relevant information from which to derive these values; and it is the traditional argument in support of the use of past acquisition costs as a basis for 'valuing' resources for reporting purposes: the so-called historic cost principle, which dominates the determination of traditional accounting income. As Kerr[5] has pointed out, it is a principle which has its roots in the 'joint venture' trading concept of the thirteenth to sixteenth centuries, when partners in a venture required an accurate accounting of the overall surplus or deficit from the venture once it had come to its end. Despite the gradual development of more permanent business enterprises, the 'cost rule'[6] in accounting has persisted, with accountants being concerned primarily with recording factual transactions based on past values. Accountants, therefore, have tended to avoid the role of valuers until the recent interest in current valuations (to be discussed in Chapter 8).

A strict adherence to the historic cost base in accounting means that accountants continue to account for resources at their original acquisition values until such time as a resource is realized; at which time, the value change is recognized. In Illustration 12, page 50, the effect of this principle may be seen clearly: the shop was acquired for £5,000, and continued to be reported at this historic cost until it was realized; at that time the value increment of £5,300 was recognized and recorded. The result of using the historic cost principle is that any unrealized gains which could be classified as income are in general ignored until such time as realization takes place. It also means that, on realization, it is inevitable that part of realized income will include gains earned in previous periods, e.g. in Illustration 12, the £5,300 capital gain on the shop sale becomes part of the income of period $t_3 - t_4$, whereas it was probably accruing throughout the previous three periods. The overall result is that the accounting income of a defined period may not be entirely representative of value changes during that period; and so the corresponding balance sheet may well portray resources expressed in outdated value terms.

This brings us to the accounting principle which is the twin of historic cost: the realization principle. As a generally accepted guideline, this formalizes the historic cost principle and advocates the recognition of income only when realization has taken place. The conversion of a resource into cash, or near cash, resources would usually constitute realization for this purpose. Realization is, however, a general rule, and there are exceptions in specific circumstances. For example, rapid rises in land and property values may lead many companies, on the grounds of the materiality of the unrealized value increments, to feel it necessary to measure and report the latter changes, even though no realization is contemplated. But on the whole, despite these exceptions, the realization principle is much adhered to in practice,[7] and, as we have seen, the overall result is that traditional accounting income for a defined period contains a heterogeneous mixture of gains of the current and prior periods (thus masking the effective income of the current period). This somewhat confusing situation can be made even more confusing by certain inconsistencies which in practice arise and are generally accepted. These occur when unrealized losses are recognized, measured and subsequently reported – the rule being that such losses should be accounted for prior to realization, whereas gains should not. There may also be inconsistencies when a significant time-lag is likely before realization eventually takes place. In these cases, such delays are accepted as reason enough for discarding the realization principle and recognizing unrealized income – the above example of revaluing properties is one instance; another would be the case of long-term contracting businesses (such as shipbuilding) where contract income can be recognized throughout the contract instead of only at the contract completion date.

While the realization approach to recognizing and reporting accounting income has been generally accepted in practice, it has also encountered a great deal of criticism over the years. It creates unnecessary delays in reporting significant items of income; it appears to be illogical in its recognition of unrealized losses but not gains; and it is subject to inconsistencies when particular circumstances are used to justify its abandonment. Several writers[8] have felt it to be an unnecessary principle which leads not only to a misleading and confusing computation of accounting income, but also to an equally misleading and confusing portrayal of resource values in the balance sheet.

The last main measurement guideline that needs to be mentioned in this section is the matching principle. Like historic cost and realization, this is in practice generally accepted by accountants, and is derived from their use. It requires that revenues which are recognized through the application of the realization principle are then related to (or matched with) relevant and appropriate historic costs. This is the generally accepted cost allocation process so important to historic cost accounting. Past costs are examined and, despite their historic nature, are subjected to a prediction-based procedure whereby cost elements regarded as having expired service potential are allocated or matched against relevant revenues. The remaining elements of cost which are regarded as continuing to have future service potential are carried forward in the traditional balance sheet and are termed as assets. Thus this last financial statement is nothing more than a report of unallocated past costs waiting expiry of their estimated future service potential before being matched with suitable revenues. The most important feature of the matching principle is that there should be some positive correlation between respective revenues and costs. There is, however, much difficulty inherent in this exercise because of the subjectiveness of the cost-allocation process which results from estimating the existence of unexpired future service potential in the historic costs concerned. A variety of allocation practices is available, and each one is capable of producing different cost aggregates to match against revenues (the main areas of difficulty affecting inventory valuation and fixed depreciation policies). Matching is, therefore, not as easy or as straightforward as it looks, and consequently much care and expertise is required to give the allocated figures sufficient credibility to satisfy their users.

## The conventional wisdoms of accounting

The preceding section describes the three main principles of accounting which inevitably result in the computation of an income measure based on caution. In other words, the measuring and reporting of traditional accounting income is usually undertaken only when its existence can be firmly evidenced by realization. Despite its faults, it is an accounting process which has survived the test of time. It has become generally accepted by the accountancy professions in the developed countries, largely because of their corresponding acceptance of the need to adhere to two main accounting conventions: conservatism and continuity.

Conservatism, or the accounting policy of reasonable caution being exercised in the measurement and reporting of income, has become so generally accepted by accountants that scarcely any explanation of its relevance and validity to income and value determination is given in the literature. It most certainly underlies the twin principles of realization and historic cost, and leads to somewhat misleading and confusing measures of periodic accounting income. It is a policy of 'not counting chickens before they are hatched' rather than of deliberate understatement of income and resource values: the accountant avoids the recognition and measurement of value changes and income until such time as they may be evidenced readily (in other words, the application of the realization principle, utilizing historic costs, is an expression of the conservatism convention in practice). This is a throw-back to the early days of accounting when the accountant was concerned to prevent management reporting an over-optimistic picture of company solvency and general financial position. It is therefore more an attitude of mind, or quality of judgement, than a measurement technique. Thus it is extremely difficult to standardize or regulate. The conservatism inherent in measures of traditional accounting income may well, therefore, vary from entity to entity, depending on the particular attitudes of the different accountants and managers concerned.

The reason for adopting the conservatism convention as part of accounting practice is not difficult to understand; it is due to the uncertainty of the future, which in turn raises doubts about the ultimate realizability of unrealized value increments. As Sterling[9] has stated, accountants are practical men who have to deal with practical problems, and so they have a tendency to avoid the somewhat speculative area of accounting for unrealized gains. They have also inherited the traditional role of acting as a curb on the enthusiasm of businessmen who want to report to ownership as successful a story as possible.

Lastly, traditional accounting reports are intended legally for stewardship purposes,[10] a function which incurs no legal obligation to report
beyond the facts of realized transactions.

So significant is conservatism in present-day accounting practice
that Sterling[11] and Arthur Andersen and Co.[12] have stated that it is a
fundamental convention which dominates all other accounting principles. For example, the historic cost principle normally ignores contemporary values and value changes (unless these are realized); and
normally the realization principle recognizes only realized gains. In
both cases, the *raison d'être* for the principle involved is, presumably,
reasoned caution resulting from the convention of conservatism.

The main reason for the continued existence and importance of
conservatism in accounting may be found in the older significant
convention of continuity or 'going concern'. This convention is, in the
accountancy literature, expressed in the form of an assumption: that
the business entity being accounted for will have an indefinite life. This
postulate is used to justify periodic reporting in accounting; the
carrying forward, sometimes indefinitely, of such unallocated past
costs representing business assets such as land and buildings; and
avoiding the valuing of non-cash resources at realization values because of uncertainty about eventual realization. As the entity is
assumed to have an indefinite and uncertain future, accountants may
have become reluctant to attempt to predict such a future (beyond
what is necessary in the cost allocation process), thus excluding, *inter
alia*, unrealized value changes, and thereby compounding their traditional conservatism, developed over the many years since the advent of
company financial reporting.

Although continuity is assumed in practically every financial accounting report, it is fair to ask whether the postulate is valid, particularly as it may contribute, albeit inadvertently, to the dubious convention of conservatism. Sterling[13] certainly doubts its validity, though the
relevant literature contains little further comment. He argues that
there is no evidence of an entity lasting in business forever. Each entity
has a limited life, ended by liquidation, acquisition or merger, and thus
continuity seems to be an invalid assumption. Sterling also makes the
perfectly justifiable comment that, whether or not the assumption or
prediction is valid, it is unnecessary since it is not really needed in
accounting to support periodic reporting, the carrying forward of
unallocated costs, or the non-use of realization values. These activities
can be conducted perfectly well by assuming a definite life for the
business entity concerned. So why should continuity be taken as such
an important aspect of traditional accounting? The probable answer is

that it can be used to justify the exclusion of unrealized value changes from financial reports (except in such well-defined circumstances as the depreciation of fixed assets), and this may well suit accountants, who are loath to become involved in such matters because of their conservative tradition. It may also be because it is a useful support for the conservatism convention and consequently helps to justify the continued use of the historic cost and realization principles.

## The defence for traditional accounting income

Many spirited advocations and defences of the traditional accounting income model have been made over the years. The most important ones have come from Kohler,[14] Littleton[15] and Ijiri,[16] and the points made in this section are drawn mainly from the writings of these accountants.

The first argument invoked to justify historic cost-based income is that it has stood the test of time and so it must have been found useful by a great many people. Yet, as Ross has stated,[17] the lack of pent-up feelings about the concept may well be due to the fact that investors and others have become used to it, can cope with it, and are unaware of the existence or merits of alternative income models.

The next favoured argument is that, since the function of accounting is to provide a knowledge of past business activity, predictions of the future can be made by using it as a foundation. In other words, the job of the accountant is to record fact rather than to value. A supporting argument to this one states that the traditional income model is credible because it is based on factual transactions which may be evidenced and verified, so that it is less open to dispute than any other income model. This is the classic defence of objectivity: that accounting income is measured and reported objectively, and that it is consequently verifiable. (The dubiety of this proposition will be discussed in the following section.)

The fact that accounting income appears well suited to two distinct managerial activities is also often used in its defence. First, it is said that it is useful for control purposes, particularly when reviewing the worth of past decisions; and secondly, it is said that it is useful for making management accountable to ownership for the use of resources entrusted to it. While these assertions may be true, such advocation tends to ignore other possible needs and requirements for income and value information which cannot be supplied by the traditional model. The defenders of historic cost-based income would then argue, however, that, because other information uses (such as decision making) require other forms of income information, this may well increase the degree of subjectiveness in accounting; which, in turn, could cause disputes because bad value judgements minimized the relevant information's reliability.

Other arguments in favour of traditional accounting income have been advanced, including one suggesting that the historic cost basis is the least costly in social and economic terms because it minimizes (a) potential disputes about information reliability; and (b) time and effort in preparing the information. An additional argument is that, in times of rising prices (which is the most usual contemporary experience), alternative income models to historic cost could give lower operating income figures, and even lower rates of return, which could lead to lower share prices and market ratings.

## Arguments against traditional accounting income

Of the several counter-arguments to the above, the main one is that the historic cost and realization principles prevent essential information about unrealized income being reported, and also lead to reports of heterogeneous mixtures of realized income items. This implies that the criteria of relevance and verity (so far as unreported information is concerned) and understandability (so far as the mixed income information is concerned) are not being complied with. It also implies that the usefulness of historic cost income may be limited to stewardship purposes and tax computations (although even these uses may not be particularly meaningful owing to the subjectivity of the underlying cost-allocation process). Arguably, therefore, traditional income may have little utility in many decision-making functions as it does not report on all income accumulated to date; it does not report contemporary values for resources; and while it reports on an income figure which contains income elements accrued in previous periods, it does so without segregating these elements. There is also an attendant danger of giving to users of financial statements the misleading impression that the traditional balance sheet is a value statement rather than merely a statement of unallocated cost balances.

As we saw previously, the traditional accounting income model is based upon conventions and principles which may be severely criticized, e.g. for the lack of very much contemporary valuation in the historic cost basis; for the unnecessary caution introduced into accounting for income by the realization principle; and for the invalid assumption of indefinite continuity in business activity. It seems obvious that each of these factors will lead to a concept of income which could be misleading, misunderstood and irrelevant to its users.

Lastly, the defences for the traditional concept are themselves open to criticism. For example, the fact that investors and others have become accustomed to using historic cost information is not, in itself, sufficient reason for retaining it as the primary income model. The fact that accountants record historic data does not mean they should ignore the process of valuation. And historic cost information is not necessarily free from potential disputes about its reliability – for example, subjective judgements are involved in the cost allocation process of matching.

## Accounting and economic incomes

The reader should by this stage be aware of the main factors attributable to the theoretical model of economic income and to the widely practised model of accounting income. It is now appropriate to examine briefly the main differences between the two models, and the worked example used throughout this chapter is given as illustration (Illustration 13). Besides the figures and information given on page 60, it is assumed that the periods are annual and that a constant 7 per cent interest rate is operative. It is also assumed, on the grounds of simplicity, that expectations in the economic model are realized exactly and are not subject to change prior to realization – in other words, a form of ideal income *ex post*. Distributions by the entity should be used as the basis for these economic value measurements in order to avoid the problem of double-counting due to reinvestment (the latter does not actually apply in this example, but the usual practice is followed nevertheless).

As the Illustration will show, the main difference between accounting income and entity economic income centres around the timing of capital value increments in the two models. The accounting income model, because it is historical and transactions based, recognizes operating flows usually only when they have been realized. On the other hand, the economic income model, because it is based on valuations of all anticipated distributions, recognizes these outflows well before they are made. This means that, at the point of original investment, economic capital will exceed accounting capital by an amount equivalent to the difference between the present value of all the anticipated distributions and the transacted value of those resources accounted for at that time. This difference represents an unrealized economic 'windfall' gain. However, it will over time be recognized and accounted for in the accounting income model as the operating cash flows are realized and accumulated prior to the final distribution on cessation of business. These subsequent realizations, already incorporated to the extent of their present value in economic capital because of prior anticipation, are then introduced into the

**Illustration 13   Comparison of accounting and economic incomes**

(a) *Accounting income*

| Period | $Y_a$* |
|--------|--------|
|        | £      |
| $t_0-t_1$ | 1,700 |
| $t_1-t_2$ | 2,200 |
| $t_2-t_3$ | 1,400 |
| $t_3-t_4$ | 5,100 |
|           | 10,400 |

\* Computed on page 50; $Y_a$ is the accounting income of the period.

(b) *Economic income (ideal ex post)*

| Period | C | $K_t$ | $K_{t-1}$ | $Y_e$* |
|--------|---|-------|-----------|--------|
|        | £ | £     | £         | £      |
| $t_0-t_1$ | — | 14,499 | 13,550 | 949 |
| $t_1-t_2$ | — | 15,514 | 14,499 | 1,015 |
| $t_2-t_3$ | — | 16,600 | 15,514 | 1,086 |
| $t_3-t_4$ | 16,600 | — | 16,600 | — |
|           | 16,600 |   |   | 3,050† |

\*   Computed as explained in Chapter 3: C is the cash distribution to PQ immediately after $t_3$ when business ceased and the shop and van had been sold; $K_t$ is the capital of the entity at the end of the period; $K_{t-1}$ is the capital of the entity at the beginning of the period; and $Y_e$ is the ideal economic income of the period.

†   In addition, there is a form of 'windfall' gain at $t_0$ amounting to £7,350 due to economic capital of £13,550 exceeding accounting capital of £6,200. (This is a form of so-called subjective goodwill due to the pre-recognition of future distributions flowing from the underlying resources in the economic model.)

$$K_0 = \frac{£16,600}{1 \cdot 07^3} \qquad K_1 = \frac{£16,600}{1 \cdot 07^2} \qquad K_2 = \frac{£16,600}{1 \cdot 07^1}$$

(c) *Comparative computation*

| Period | $Y_a{}^*$ £ | + | $\Delta$SGW £ | = | $Y_e{}^*$ £ | + | W £ |
|--------|------|---|------|---|------|---|-----|
| $t_0-t_0$ | — | | $7,350^{(a)}$ | | — | | 7,350 |
| $t_0-t_1$ | 1,700 | | $(751)^{(b)}$ | | 949 | | — |
| $t_1-t_2$ | 2,200 | | $(1,185)^{(c)}$ | | 1,015 | | — |
| $t_2-t_3$ | 1,400 | | $(314)^{(d)}$ | | 1,086 | | — |
| $t_3-t_4$ | 5,100 | | $(5,100)^{(e)}$ | | — | | — |
| | 10,400 | | | | 3,050 | | 7,350 |

* as in (a) and (b)

$Y_a$ is the accounting income of the defined periods.

$\Delta$SGW is the change in value of subjective goodwill – initially, as it is created in an unrealized form due to the pre-recognition in the economic model of cash distributions resulting from business activity; and subsequently, due to its gradual diminution in economic value as it is realized within the accounting model.

W is a 'windfall' gain accruing at $t_0$ owing to the excess of economic capital value over the equivalent accounting figure at that point in time (in other words, it is due to the pre-recognition of future cash distributions from the entity).

The following computations support the above figures and explanations.
(a)  economic capital ($t_0$) – accounting capital ($t_0$); £13,550–6,200
(b)  [economic capital ($t_1$) – accounting capital ($t_1$)] – [economic capital ($t_0$) – accounting capital ($t_0$)]; [£14,499–7,900] – [£13,550–6,200]
(c)  [economic capital ($t_2$) – accounting capital ($t_2$)] – [economic capital ($t_1$) – accounting capital ($t_1$)]; [£15,514–10,100] – [£14,499–7,900]
(d)  [economic capital ($t_3$) – accounting capital ($t_3$)] – [economic capital ($t_2$) – accounting capital ($t_2$)]; [£16,600–11,500] – [£15,514–10,100]
(e)  [economic capital ($t_4$) – accounting capital ($t_4$)] – [economic capital ($t_3$) – accounting capital ($t_3$)]; [£0–0] – [£16,600–11,500]

corresponding accounting model. Thus, the unrealized difference between economic and accounting capitals at the time of original investment is gradually amortized until the two figures equate at the time of disinvestment. The figures therefore reveal that the periodic differences between accounting and economic income result from unrealized and realized gains which appear in one model and not in the other for the reasons just stated. They are denoted as $\Delta$SGW in the computations given in Illustration 13.

The comparison of economic and accounting incomes in the Illustration follows the format identified by both Solomons[18] and Hansen;[19] i.e. periodic accounting income, plus unrealized value changes in economic capital accruing in the period and not accounted for in the accounting income model, less value changes in economic capital realized in the period, accruing in previous periods and not accounted for in the accounting model, lead to periodic economic income if this includes the initial 'windfall' gain. In the accounting income model, account is therefore taken of value changes in accounting capital when they are normally realized and in the period of realization; and irrespective of when they were accruing (there are exceptions to this generalization – as in fixed asset depreciation). In Illustration 12, for example, the increase in the value of the shop was accounted for only when the shop was sold; and the decrease in the value of the van was recognized piecemeal through the application of the depreciation policy. Thus, periodic accounting income invariably includes gains accruing in previous periods. On the other hand, the economic income model anticipates capital value changes whenever they accrue. In Illustration 13, the present value of economic capital to $t_0$ was based upon the eventual distribution to the owner, thereby resulting in the 'windfall' gain. Subsequent economic income arose because the value of economic capital increased as a result of the pending realization of cash flows to which it was related. At no time does economic income include a realized gain which accrued in a previous period.

The nature of the 'windfall' element at $t_0$, so-called subjective goodwill, is worth some additional comment before we go further. As was seen in Chapter 3, the economic value at the original point of investment in the various economic models differs from the actual cost of investment. There is therefore the problem of how to treat the 'windfall' for income purposes – is it capital, income or a mixture of both? It arises in this case because the economic model recognizes, as soon as they can be predicted, the cash distributions which result from operating cash flows which will eventually be recognized for accounting purposes. In the traditional accounting model, it is realized and incorporated into the periodic income measures, and thus capital is maintained at its original cost of £6,200 (£5,000 for the shop and £1,200 for the van). In the economic model, if it is treated entirely as income, capital would be maintained at £6,200, as in the accounting model. However, this would assume that the owner did not wish to maintain his capital at a level allowing for the possible replacement of tangible resources at values different from the original cost, or for the possible replacement by purchase of his own skills and experience. To treat the 'windfall' gain entirely as capital would alleviate some of the doubts pertaining to future replacement and maintenance of capital and income, but would ignore the possibility of the owner still having the 'free' use of his own skills and experience. Therefore the 'windfall' may well contain elements of both income and capital, depending on what assumptions are made with regard to capital maintenance. For the sake of simplicity and practical realism in the example cited, the 'windfall' of £7,350 is hereafter regarded as a capital adjustment rather than as income. This is also done to contrast for the reader the alternative approach of income treatment used in Chapter 3.

Overall, therefore, total accounting income equals total economic income, if 'windfall' gains are added to the latter figure. But the main difference in the periodic figures is the recognition of unrealized changes in capital value only in the economic model. Accounting income takes value changes into account usually when they are realized. It therefore includes the eventual realizations of the initial 'windfall' gain recognized at the point of original investment in the economic model. It is important, therefore, that the inclusion of these 'windfall' elements in traditional accounting income be recognized so as to prevent possible overconsumption through distributions, etc., should the whole or part of the 'windfall' be regarded as having a capital nature. The reason for the difference in the treatment of the realization of value increments has been met already – the accountant essentially adopts a totally backward-looking or *ex post* approach, and consequently ignores potential capital value changes; the economist, by contrast, is forward-looking in his model and bases his capital value on future events. The most significant difference between the two models, therefore, is one of realization – the economist basing his model on unrealized value changes while the accountant, in the main, bases his model on those benefits which have been realized. This is natural enough, when it is considered that the accounting model is intended to be transactions based, in contrast to the economic model, which is predictions based. It also means that, whereas the accountant is striving for objectivity maximization to produce a reliable measure of income for reporting purposes, the economist is free of such a constraint and is quite content in his model to put up with large-scale subjectivity. After all, he is not concerned with reporting an entity activity; he is simply using his model as a tool for analysis in microeconomic theory. As a result, the two income concepts appear to be poles apart in concept and measurement – certainly the accountant would find the economic model almost impossible to put into practice in financial reporting, despite its eminently desirable theoretical qualities; and the economist would fail to find much relevance in the accounting model as a 'guide to prudent personal conduct'. The following few chapters therefore look at income models which attempt to incorporate economic thinking into the accounting model without making it wholly prediction based. In particular, the emphasis on unrealized value changes in these alternative models will be noticeable.

## References

(See pages 177–8 for Selected Bibliography)

1. R. R. Sterling, 'Conservatism: the Fundamental Principle of Valuation in Traditional Accounting', *Abacus,* December 1967, p. 110.

2. J. B. Canning, *The Economics of Accountancy – a Critical Analysis of Accounting Theory,* The Ronald Press, 1929, p. 161.

3. See A. L. Thomas, 'The Allocation Problem in Financial Accounting Theory', *Studies in Accounting Research 3,* American Accounting Association, 1969.

4. S. Gilman, *Accounting Concepts of Profit,* The Ronald Press, 1939, pp. 55–6.

5. J. St. G. Kerr, 'Three Concepts of Business Income', *Australian Accountant,* April 1956, p. 141.

6. Phrase attributed to Sterling in his various writings.

7. It is to be evidenced in the relevant legislative and professional accounting provisions of most developed countries.

8. For example, J. H. Myers, 'The Critical Event and Recognition of Net Profit', *Accounting Review,* October 1959, pp. 528–32; American Accounting Association Committee, 'The Realization Concept', *Accounting Review,* April 1965, pp. 312–22; and C. T. Horngren, 'How Should We Interpret the Realization Concept?', *Accounting Review,* April 1965, pp. 323–33.

9. Sterling, 'Conservatism', op. cit., p. 109.

10. ibid.

11. ibid.

12. Arthur Andersen and Co., *Objectives of Financial Statements for Business Enterprises,* Arthur Andersen & Co., 1972, p. 37.

13. Sterling, op. cit., p. 130.

14. E. L. Kohler, 'Why Not Retain Historical Cost?', *Journal of Accountancy,* October 1963, pp. 35–41.

15. A. C. Littleton, 'The Significance of Invested Cost', *Accounting Review,* April 1952, pp. 167–73.

16. Y. Ijiri, 'A Defence of Historical Cost Accounting', in R. R. Sterling (ed.), *Asset Valuation and Income Determination,* Scholars Book Co., 1971, pp. 1–14.

17. H. Ross, *Financial Statements – A Crusade for Current Values,* Pitman, 1969, pp. 19–20.

18. D. Solomons, 'Economic and Accounting Concepts of Income', *Accounting Review,* July 1961, pp. 374–83.

19. P. Hansen, *The Accounting Concept of Profit,* North-Holland Publishing, 1962, pp. 57–63.

# 5 Current value concepts of income

## Introduction

The previous two chapters have described two distinct extremes in the area of income and value determination: the 'ultra confident' economic model which anticipates income and value changes; and the 'ultra cautious' accounting model which ignores value changes unless they are evidenced as realized. Ideally, the economic model is the one which seems to have the greatest relevance to decision makers, because of its emphasis on the future and the factors of present value, consumption and reinvestment. Its practicality is, however, negated by its measurement approach based on prediction. Despite this 'fault', it contains several ideas which many accountants are becoming increasingly interested in – particularly its lack of adherence to the realization principle, and its consequent recognition of contemporary values, value changes and unrealized income. Historic cost accounting income, on the other hand, has the significant merit of being based upon verifiable transactions. It is not surprising, therefore, that interest in alternative income models which incorporate the more favourable elements of both the economic and traditional accounting income models – particularly, the combination of current values and the transactions base – should be mounting. Thus, the current value income school has emerged, supporting income models which recognize current values and value changes, realized and unrealized income, and current and prior period income; besides adhering to the necessary income criteria which affect practical measurement and communication for reporting purposes.

Current value models are based upon current market values which are incorporated into the traditional process of recognizing and recording past transactions. Thus, in the fundamental accounting income identity (defined in Chapter 1, page 6) of $Y_a = D + (R_t - R_{t-1})$, residual equities $R_t$ and $R_{t-1}$ would be re-expressed in current value terms, and accounting income $Y_a$ would become a mixture of realized and un-realized gains of the current period. The accounting process therefore does not abandon the objectivity of recorded transactions. But it does require that, when past values become outmoded owing to the passing of time, appropriate valuation adjustments be made to re-express the assets and liabilities underlying residual equity in contemporary terms. Thus the most beneficial feature of traditional accounting is retained, and the income and value concepts more important to the economic model are incorporated (e.g. the recognition of unrealized value changes).

The computation of current value income will be explained in detail in the chapters which follow, but the reader should be aware of the undernoted identities and relationships in the meantime.

Current value income $Y_c$ consists of two elements, both *accruing* in the current period of reporting: realized income RY and unrealized income UY. Therefore, in any defined period, $Y_c = RY + UY$. Similarly, traditional accounting income $Y_a$ is comprised of two elements, each of which is *realized* in the current period of reporting: accrued income of the period RY and accrued income of previous periods RY'. (This mixture of income was explained in Chapter 4.) Therefore, in any defined period, $Y_a = RY + RY'$. There is thus an element of RY common to each income identity, and so, by deducting the unrealized element UY and adding the prior year element RY' to current value income $Y_c$, $Y_a$ may be derived as follows, $Y_c - UY + RY' = Y_a$. This is one of the major advantages of the current value models; they not only provide relevant information which the traditional accounting model ignores, but are also capable of adaptation to the latter model should this be necessary for reporting purposes.

The next point to be noted at this introductory stage concerns the nature of current market values. In effect, there are two main alternatives: *current acquisition values*, or entry prices, which represent the current cost of replacing the resources underlying accounting capital; and *current realization values*, or exit prices, which represent the proceeds which would be realized should such resources be sold at the present time. These two alternatives thus give rise to two distinct current value income models, each of which comprise the subject of a later chapter: entry prices, which form the basis of business income; and exit values, which form the basis of realizable income.

It should also be noted that, in recent years, a third alternative current value model has received considerable support. Based on Bonbright's 'value to the owner' concept[1] (since renamed 'deprival value' – the maximum loss a business would suffer if deprived of the asset concerned), this model utilizes a mixture of entry, exit and economic values – each within well-defined circumstances. This approach forms the basis of current cost accounting which will be described in Chapter 8.

## Arguments for current value income

Detailed cases for current value based income have been made occasionally over many years,[2] but only recently have the arguments been sustained. The following summarizes the main arguments being put forward in what is still a developing debate.

The fact that traditional accounting for income to a great extent ignores current values and value changes, and so ignores significant information about entity wealth and progress, is often put forward as the main argument to support current value income. As many writers have stated, the user of financial statements should be interested in the current state of an entity's affairs, and these should be expressed in contemporary terms. To express these matters in historic terms (i.e. based on past acquisition costs) is, according to MacNeal,[3] to ignore truth in accounting. Past costs do not reflect current values, and yet the traditional balance sheet, expressed in historic cost terms, implies a statement of current values. It can hardly be said to correspond to the criterion of verity advocated by Sterling.[4]

Besides ignoring contemporary values of relevance to the user of financial statements, the traditional accounting model also ignores value changes unless they are realized. This raises the problems, already mentioned, of unrealized income being ignored and of heterogeneous income being reported. The result is a misleading and confusing portrayal of entity income which is not particularly useful or beneficial. Truth and reality are therefore obscured in the traditional income model, and current value accounting, it is argued, could minimize these faults by presenting contemporary values, reporting unrealized gains and segregating prior period from current period income elements.

Another leading argument for current value income involves the requirement that income and value information should be of relevance to those users of financial statements concerned mainly with using it to help them in decision making activities. Most persons and bodies interested in the economic affairs of individual business entities need to make decisions affecting their interest or relationship with the entities. Over the years, measures of entity income and value have been found exceptionally useful in making such decisions. Decision makers therefore need information that will help them to determine alternative courses of action, predict the consequences of such alternatives and select preferred courses of action. In general, it is agreed that data reflecting present prices, position and progress are most relevant for these purposes. Yet, traditional accounting information on income and value, even though it does not fully reflect the current states of entities, has had to be, and continues to be, used in decision making as well as in its intended stewardship role. Current value information nevertheless has greater relevance to decision activities than historic cost information.

As mentioned above, the ideal information to aid decision makers seems to be that which derives from the economic income model. In particular, the latter's emphasis on the future is highly relevant to the taking of decisions concerned with alternative courses of action and economic behaviour. But, because of its lack of practicality, economic income is not an ideal concept for reporting purposes, and so a number of accountants[5] have argued for an income model which is an acceptable surrogate for economic income. Staubus, in particular, has advocated this use of current value accounting on the grounds that current values are an indication of the future cash flows which are essential elements of the economic model based on measurements of discounted future benefits – e.g. disposal values are obvious indicators of cash flows. It should be noted, however, that the current value income models are not identical or equivalent to the economic models, even though they have common features. In this connection, the current value models can only describe minimum 'present values' in situations where resources are held because their economic value is greater than their replacement cost or net realizable value. What is lacking, therefore, in the current value models is the 'windfall' element: the so-called subjective goodwill, representing the difference between the economic value of the entity and its resources, and its current market value expressed in terms of either replacement costs or net realizable values. This difference is one of the major weaknesses of the current value models, and results from the lack of recognition, *inter alia*, of significant intangible resources of the entity. (This will be discussed further in Chapters 6, 7, 8 and 9.) For this reason, current value models should normally be thought of as alternative measures of entity income rather than as substitutes for economic measures which have such practical frailty.

One of the most considerable criticisms of traditional accounting income information is its inability to allow its user to differentiate between operational gains, over which management should normally have a great deal of control, and gains due to holding assets, many of which may be outside such control. Accounting income, being generally expressed as an aggregate figure, does not make this distinction, and so raises problems for a decision maker interested in assessing and predicting the quality of entity management. In addition, the decision maker has little idea of how much of the aggregate income figure accrued in the current period under review, and how much accrued in prior periods. He is therefore deprived of vital information with which to assess the operational and other activity of the current period. The current value models, on the other hand, do attempt to separate operational from holding gains, and current from prior period accounting income. They do not suffer from the faults of the realization principle, and therefore, it is argued by the advocates of current value, they provide much more meaningful and relevant information to decision makers since they make these vital informational distinctions.

In Chapter 4 the main principles and conventions of traditional accounting were discussed at length. In particular, it was seen that it is the convention of conservatism which gives rise to most of the points of criticism mentioned in previous paragraphs – e.g. the non-disclosure of unrealized income and the lack of segregation of income elements. It was also suggested that the convention of continuity was a questionable assumption. All this leads to the conclusion that the measurement foundations on which traditional accounting is built are somewhat outmoded. For this reason, the alternative current value models are cited as alternatives which, because of their adherence to contemporary values and value changes, are not based on these dubious principles and conventions.

In the function of decision making, constant comparisons need to be made, either intra- or inter-entity, so as to assess the relative progress of a particular entity over time, or to assess the progress of one entity in comparison with that of another. It is therefore essential that the accounting information used for this purpose be capable of allowing for the making of reasonable comparisons. It may be argued that information relating to the traditional accounting income model is not satisfactorily comparable because of its use of a heterogeneous mixture of past acquisition costs. These can lead to entirely different measures of income and capital for what are essentially similar types of entity, i.e. to differences arising because of differences in the acquisition dates of similar resources underlying capital. Such a situation is obviously not satisfactory, and advocates of current value income point out that, despite dissimilarities in business activity, the accounting data of different entities are rendered more meaningful for comparative purposes by the use of values derived at a similar point in time. This would at least avoid the unnecessary complication of comparing data which were based upon values derived at different points of time.

## Arguments against current value income

Various counter-arguments to the arguments in favour of current value income have, of course, been put forward from time to time. The first concerns the view that accountants are primarily recorders rather than valuers: that the accountant's job is to record factual transactions in the value terms relevant to them at the time of transacting. Since this is so, the argument runs, these factual records will become 'submerged' in a variety of value adjustments, thereby concealing valuable steward-ship information. But this particular standpoint ignores the fact that the current value income models do not preclude the reporting of historic cost income. Indeed, as we have seen, the latter income figure may be derived from the former since each utilizes the same historic transactions base.

The second counter-argument suggests that current value based accounting is somehow less objective and verifiable than the tradi-tional accounting model. The feeling behind this proposition is that the process of valuation is subjective and so involves a great deal of personal judgement. This would not, however, be the case in the majority of instances where established and generally known market prices are available for use as the basis to determine current values.

The familiar argument that the historic cost concept of income has stood the so-called test of time has also been invoked to criticize the advocation of current value income: in other words, a cry for the *status quo*. This follows the traditionally cautious approach of accountants, which could therefore mean that useful and relevant information for decision-making purposes was being ignored.

The remaining counter-arguments have mainly concerned technical points to do with the computation of current value income. These question the assumptions underlying the use of particular current values – e.g. (a) that the use of entry or replacement costs assumes that the resources concerned are going to be replaced, and that the form of replacement is known with some degree of certainty; or, alternatively, (b) that the use of exit or net realizable values assumes that the resources, or, indeed, the entity itself, are going to be liquidated. Both these points centre on aspects of business activity which make the prediction of resource replacement or realization a very uncertain affair. Within the context of normal business behaviour, however, neither resource replacement nor realization appear to be invalid assumptions to make. The uncertainty relating to the eventual replacement or realization values does make the current value models vulnerable to such criticism, however.

## The alternative current value models

The alternative income models have already been outlined on page 25: $Y_e$ economic income, $Y_a$ accounting income, $Y_b$ business income, $Y_r$ realizable income, and $Y_{cc}$ current cost income. Of these, $Y_b$, $Y_r$ and $Y_{cc}$ constitute the alternative current value models. Each is based on a different concept of current value: business income on replacement cost, realizable income on realizable value, and current cost income on deprival value. Therefore each is capable of producing different income figures. It is important that these differences in current valuation accounting should be understood.

To begin with, business, realizable and current cost incomes are not competing alternatives in the field of income and value determination; i.e. they are not competing against each other, or against economic or traditional accounting income, for the title of 'best' income concept. There is, in fact, no such thing as the 'best' concept; each model has its own particular uses, advantages and disadvantages. Business, realizable and current cost incomes, although each is current value based, are therefore separate models which should be looked on as being useful for specific purposes. This view is contrary to another,[6] which states that current values should be used as surrogates for present values in the economic income model, meaning that realizable values should be used for resources which are going to be sold, and replacement costs for those which are going to be held for use. Such a viewpoint of current valuation ignores the fact that the alternative current value models produce income measures which have a usefulness and relevance in their own right, in much the same way as economic income.

## Difficulties of current valuation

Before we go on to explain in detail the processes involved in current value measurements, it seems appropriate to mention briefly that, while the three relevant models are mainly market price based, it is not always easy to determine these market prices. For example, there may not be a ready market to refer to (as in the case of such intangible resources as goodwill) or a market which is representative of values over a period of time (as in the case of demand far exceeding the available supply owing to temporary shortages). For this reason, the following points should be kept to closely when current values are used: (a) such values as are used must be objective commercial values, not imaginary ones; (b) the values concerned should preferably only refer to 'normal' quantities of the relevant resources rather than those which are affected by exceptional bulk purchasing and selling (this is particularly the case with inventories), but much must depend on what is 'normal' in the circumstances of a particular entity; and (c) the markets in which the values are determined should, ideally, be free, active and representative of the resources and transactions in which the entity concerned is involved.

## Current values and price-level restatement

To restate briefly the point made in general terms at the end of the introductory Chapter 1: current valuation is a value process necessary to determine capital for income purposes, whereas price-level restatement is a separate process to determine the amount of capital to be maintained and the proportion of the value increment to be treated as income. It seems possible that this distinction is not always clear in the minds of accountants, who may unjustifiably regard price-level restatement as a valuation process, and therefore as a substitute for current value accounting. As has already been pointed out, the process of price-level restatement can be applied to all the value models (past, current or future).

The confusion could potentially arise mainly in connection with the price-level restatement of historic cost data. It might be believed that accounting income, adjusted in this way, is in some way equivalent to current value income. This is not the case. A general price-level series of adjustments to historic cost income still leaves its user with historic cost income based on past values. All that has been done is to reflect, in the reported information, any variations resulting from changes in the value of the monetary measuring unit. Only by accident will price-level adjusted historic data approximate to current values. Current value income, unlike traditional accounting income, recognizes contemporary value changes before realization. This is something that price-level adjusted accounting income cannot be said to do.

# References

(See page 178 for Selected Bibliography)

1. J. C. Bonbright, *The Valuation of Property*, McGraw-Hill, 1937, p. 71.

2. For example, K. MacNeal, *Truth in Accounting*, Scholars Book Co., 1970 (reprint); E. O. Edwards and P. W. Bell, *The Theory and Measurement of Business Income*, University of California Press, 1961; and H. Ross, *Financial Statements – A Crusade for Current Values*, Pitman, 1969.

3. MacNeal, *Truth in Accounting*.

4. R. R. Sterling, *Theory of the Measurement of Enterprise Income*, University of Kansas Press, 1970, p. 41.

5. For example, G. J. Staubus, 'The Relevance of Evidence of Cash Flows', in R. R. Sterling (ed.), *Asset Valuation and Income Determination – a Consideration of Alternatives*, Scholars Book Co., 1971, pp. 42–69.

6. ibid.

# 6 Current entry values and business income

## The case for entry values

The case for current value income, based upon entry prices or values, has been advocated by many writers over the years. The main current school of thought, however, stems from the work of Edwards and Bell,[1] first published in 1961, while other major contributions in the area have come subsequently from the American Accounting Association,[2] Sprouse and Moonitz,[3] and Revsine.[4] The purpose of the present chapter is to examine in some detail the entry value model, utilizing the format laid down by Edwards and Bell. Apart from the fact that accounting information in the entry value model describes income, value and capital in contemporary terms, the main reason for its advocation is to facilitate the evaluation of past decisions by management and the formulation of future decisions – i.e. (a) operational decisions involving the processing and subsequent sale of goods and services; and (b) holding decisions involving the holding of resources over time as their pre-realization value changes. The entry value model therefore seems to have greatest relevance to entity management, which is obviously concerned with making these evaluations. It is, however, also of relevance to the investor and other external interests who may wish to evaluate managerial performance in relation to the aggregate and separable effects of these two categories of decision. As will be shown, entry value-based income distinguishes operating and holding gains even though it is now generally recognized that these are interdependent as a result of joint decisions regarding the acquisition and use of the assets concerned.[5]

In order to produce data which segregate the financial consequences of operational and holding activities, the current value adopted in this chapter is replacement cost. The use of this value has been justified on the grounds that, until an asset leaves the entity as a result of a sale, its entry value to the entity is the only relevant one.[6] It has also been recently justified[7] in terms of its approximation to the deprival value of an entity's assets in almost all circumstances (deprival value being defined as the maximum loss the entity would suffer if it were deprived of its assets).

The replacement cost basis for income determination thus attempts to reflect changes in entity capital at the point of realization in operational activity, and, before realization, in the process of holding. Thus, entry value income not only utilizes current values and segregates operational from holding income, but also abandons the realization principle which is such a major element of traditional accounting practice. As an income model, it therefore goes much further than the piecemeal attempts at producing current value income without adopting a full system of current value accounting – e.g. as in the use of the last in, first out basis for inventory accounting, or replacement cost depreciation, or occasional revaluations of certain fixed assets.

## The concept of business income

The concept of business income (income based upon replacement costs) was advocated originally by Edwards and Bell,[8] but has been advocated by others, some of whom[9] prefer to describe it as money income. For the purposes of this text, however, the original Edwards and Bell term and definition will be used. The object of this section is to explain the constituent parts of business income before going on to describe its measurement in detail, and the simplest way to start is with traditional accounting income. It should be noted that the computations and explanations which follow are not intended to replicate the work of Edwards and Bell, nor will they make any judgement as to the relevance of business income measurements (or any of its components) at this stage.

As has been explained in Chapter 4 (pages 52–4), accounting income is a heterogeneous mixture of current and prior year gains, computed by comparing sales revenues with relevant matched historic costs. This means that it effectively includes two types of gain: (a) the realized operating gain at time of sale, representing the profit received by the entity over and above the current replacement costs of the resources concerned; and (b) the realized holding gains at time of sale, representing the increase in replacement costs of the resources concerned during the period they were held prior to sale. The holding gains can in turn be divided into two elements: (a) those which accrued and were realized during the current period of reporting; and (b) those which were realized during the current period but which accrued in prior periods. Accounting income can therefore be identified as: $Y_a = COP+RHG+RHG'$; where $Y_a$ is the accounting income of the period; COP is the current operating profit of the period; RHG are the realized and accrued holding gains of the period; and RHG' are the realized holding gains of the period, accruing in previous periods. This analysis can be demonstrated by a simple example.

Assume 1,000 units of inventory were purchased at $t_0$ for £1,000. At $t_1$ their replacement cost was £1,500, and at $t_2$ their replacement cost was £1,800, at which time they were sold for £2,000.

Traditional accounting would not recognize any income from these transactions until the period $t_1-t_2$ when accounting income would be measured as the sale proceeds minus the original cost – i.e. £2,000–1,000 = £1,000. Following the above analysis, it can be seen that the accounting income figure is made up of three parts, as specified above: COP is £2,000–1,800 = £200; RHG is £1,800–1,500 = £300; RHG' is £1,500–1,000 = £500; and, therefore $Y_a$ is £200+300+500 = £1,000. It therefore seems relatively obvious that the traditional measurement of accounting income does not segregate it into its constituent parts, which means that significant information is 'hidden' in the aggregate figure. Business income attempts to remove this problem of the non-segregation of operating from holding gains, and of current from prior period gains.

Business income bases its measurements on replacement costs, and this being so recognizes current period income in both its realized and unrealized forms. It comprises the two types of gain mentioned and defined above: current operating profit of the current period (COP) and holding gains of the same period (i.e. realized gains (RHG) and also unrealized gains (UHG)). The last type of gain is represented by the change in a resource's replacement cost prior to realization. Thus, business income is identified as follows: $Y_b = COP+RHG+UHG$; where $Y_b$ is the business income; and the remaining notation is as defined above. Using the above example, the computation of business income can be shown as follows:

In period $t_0-t_1$, COP is nil, as is RHG, but UHG amounts to £1,500–1,000 = £500. Therefore, $Y_b$ for period $t_0-t_1$, would be £500. In period $t_1-t_2$, COP would be £2,000–1,800 = £200, and RHG would be £1,800–1,500 = £300. There are no unrealized gains in this period. Therefore, $Y_b$ for period $t_1-t_2$ would be £200+£300 = £500.

**Illustration 14  Accounting and business incomes**

| Period | COP [1] £ | RHG [2] £ | UHG [3] £ | RHG' [4] £ | $Y_a$ [1]+[2]+[4] £ | $Y_b$ [1]+[2]+[3] £ |
|--------|------|------|------|------|------|------|
| $t_0-t_1$ | — | — | 500 | — | — | 500 |
| $t_1-t_2$ | 200 | 300 | — | 500 | 1,000 | 500 |
|  | 200 | 300 | 500 | 500 | 1,000 | 1,000 |

Using this example, it is possible to make the comparison given in Illustration 14 (notation as defined above). Thus, in total, $Y_a$ identifies with $Y_b$ once all gains are realized, but $Y_b$ anticipates and reports holding gains prior to realization, whereas this is not the case with $Y_a$. The essential difference is therefore one of realization; and business income does not adhere to this traditional accounting principle. The two concepts of income may therefore be identified and reconciled as follows:

$$Y_a = COP + RHG + RHG'$$
$$Y_b = COP + RHG + UHG$$
Therefore, $Y_b - UHG + RHG' = Y_a$

The convenience of the business income model may be immediately seen: not only does it compute a segregated income measure for the period of reporting, but it also enables traditional accounting income to be derived from it by eliminating unrealized holding gains and adding realized holding gains accrued in previous periods. The traditional accounting model need not therefore be abandoned, neither need the historic transactions base. Indeed, the latter is required for business income computations as much as it is for accounting income.

Before going further into the computation of business income, one final point must be mentioned. The replacement cost based income model has introduced us to the concept of the holding gain. Up till now in the text, however, the nature of such holding gains has not been subjected to much comment. In fact, there are three distinct types of holding gain, each depending on the nature of the resources to which they relate. For purposes of simplifying the explanations in this text, these are described as inventory holding gains (representing realized and unrealized changes in the replacement cost of inventories of raw materials, semi-processed goods and finished goods); fixed asset cost savings (representing realized and unrealized changes in the replacement cost of depreciated fixed assets); and capital gains (representing realized and unrealized changes in the replacement cost of undepreciated fixed assets). Each of these elements of holding gain may appear in the business and accounting income computations, and all three are likely to occur in manufacturing businesses in particular.

## Business income in practice

The preceding section has given the reader a brief introduction to the concept of business income and its main elements. The present section is, in contrast, intended to explain the process of computing these factors. The figures on accounting income already utilized in Chapter 4 will be used once again: i.e. a business opened at $t_0$ with the purchase of a motor van for £1,200 and a shop for £5,000; cash operating surpluses before depreciation were £2,000 (period $t_0-t_1$), £2,500 (period $t_1-t_2$) and £1,700 (period $t_2-t_3$); realization of the van and shop, immediately after $t_3$, was for £100 and £10,300 respectively when business operations ceased; and the use of a straight-line depreciation policy for the van over four years with an estimated nil scrap value. In addition, the following replacement costs existed at each relevant date: at $t_1$, van £1,400 and shop £6,000; at $t_2$, van £1,700 and shop £7,500; and at $t_3$, van £1,800 and shop £10,000. As there is no inventory, the holding gains will be fixed asset cost savings and capital gains. It has been assumed that the replacement costs for the van refer to a new rather than to a used vehicle, thus necessitating appropriate adjustments for replacement cost depreciation underprovided in previous years. The alternative assumption of replacement costs for a used vehicle would not, however, alter the underlying income measurement principles. The same valuation distinction can be made with respect to undepreciated resources, such as the shop, but this makes no difference to the measurement details due to the lack of depreciation provisions.

In addition, it should be noted that the replacement costs of the van and the shop can either be thought of in terms of identical or equivalent resources. In many instances it is impossible to establish replacement costs for identical assets due to the uniqueness of certain resources (such as land and buildings) or technological change (as with plant and equipment). This problem will be discussed further on in the chapter but, in the meantime, it is not essential to the undernoted computations and explanations to state which approach has been adopted.

Illustration 15 follows the computational process in detail, and the following explanations provide a commentary on the computations (a) to (h).

**Illustration 15 Computation of business income**
(a) *Current operating profits*

|  | Period | | | | |
|---|---|---|---|---|---|
|  | $t_0-t_1$ £ | $t_1-t_2$ £ | $t_2-t_3$ £ | $t_3-t_4$ £ | Total £ |
| Income before depreciation | 2,000 | 2,500 | 1,700 | — | 6,200 |
| *Less:* replacement cost depreciation | 350[a] | 425[b] | 450[c] | 350[d] | 1,575 |
| *Current operating profits* | 1,650 | 2,075 | 1,250 | (350) | 4,625 |

(a) $\frac{1}{4}\times£1,400$; (b) $\frac{1}{4}\times£1,700$; (c) $\frac{1}{4}\times£1,800$; (d) $\frac{1}{4}\times£1,800-£100$

*Illustration 15a:* Current operating profits have been measured by taking the trading income for each period (assumed to be expressed in current value terms) and, from it, deducting depreciation on the motor van in current replacement cost terms. Thus, current operating profit is measured consistently in current value terms for all revenues and matched costs.

(b) *Cost savings of current period*

|  | Period | | | | |
|---|---|---|---|---|---|
|  | $t_0-t_1$ £ | $t_1-t_2$ £ | $t_2-t_3$ £ | $t_3-t_4$ £ | Total £ |
| Increase in replacement cost of van | 200[a] | 300[b] | 100[c] | — | 600 |
| *Less:* realized cost savings of period | 50[d] | 75[e] | 25[f] | — | 150 |
|  | 150 | 225 | 75 | — | 450 |
| *Less:* underprovided replacement cost depreciation in previous years | — | 75[g] | 50[h] | — | 125 |
| *Unrealized cost savings of period* | 150[i] | 150[j] | 25[k] | — | 325 |

(a) $£1,400-1,200$; (b) $£1,700-1,400$; (c) $£1,800-1,700$; (d) $\frac{1}{4}\times£200$; (e) $\frac{1}{4}\times£300$; (f) $\frac{1}{4}\times£100$; (g) $\frac{1}{4}\times£300$; (h) $2\times\frac{1}{4}\times£100$; (i) $3\times\frac{1}{4}\times£200$; (j) $2\times\frac{1}{4}\times£300$; (k) $1\times\frac{1}{4}\times£100$.

*Illustration 15b:*   Cost savings represent holding gains or 'savings' which an entity enjoys by having purchased a depreciable fixed asset at a cost which is less than it would have been if the entity had had to buy it currently. (This assumes the normal situation of rising prices; the reverse is applicable if prices are falling.) Thus, the entity gains because the historic cost depreciation it charges against operating income is less than that computed on a current replacement cost basis. When the replacement cost of a depreciable fixed asset increases, this results in an unrealized holding gain; a portion of which will be treated as realized in the period in which it arises owing to its being written off as part of the replacement cost depreciation charge. The appropriate proportion written off depends on the percentage of resource cost being depreciated in each period. Both the realized and unrealized cost savings, are, however, holding gains which are treated as part of the business income of the current period. They represent that part of traditional accounting income which arises as a result of gains resulting from the purchase of depreciable fixed assets at historic costs below the level of current costs (again assuming rising prices). The under-provision of replacement cost depreciation in previous years arises from the use of replacement costs of a new rather than second-hand van, and would be deducted from its gross replacement cost in each appropriate adjusted balance sheet. (In recent practice, at least within the UK, this underprovision has been described as 'backlog' depreciation.)

(c) *Realized cost savings of prior periods*

|  | Period | | | | |
| --- | --- | --- | --- | --- | --- |
|  | $t_0-t_1$ £ | $t_1-t_2$ £ | $t_2-t_3$ £ | $t_3-t_4$ £ | Total £ |
| Unrealized cost savings of period | 150 | 150 | 25 | — | 325 |
| Realized in period $t_1-t_2$ |  | 50[a] |  |  | 50 |
| $t_2-t_3$ |  |  | 50[a] |  |  |
|  |  |  | 75[b] |  | 125 |
| $t_3-t_4$ |  |  |  | 50[a] |  |
|  |  |  |  | 75[b] |  |
|  |  |  |  | 25[c] | 150 |
| *Realized cost savings of prior periods* | — | 50 | 125 | 150 | 325 |

(a) $\frac{1}{2}\times£150$; (b) $\frac{1}{2}\times£150$; (c) $1\times£25$

*Illustration 15c:* The cost savings which arise as explained above will eventually be realized in total through the normal process of depreciation over the useful life of the fixed assets concerned. Therefore, the unrealized gains mentioned in (b) will be realized in subsequent periods. They are realized in a sequence corresponding to that used in the allocation of resource costs by depreciation. Such realized gains are not elements of business income of the period in which they are realized; they therefore do not enter into the business income computation (however, they already have been computed as part of the business incomes of prior periods in their unrealized form). Despite this, they do form part of traditional accounting income which is based solely on realized gains. Indeed, the realized cost savings of a current period, together with the realized cost savings of prior periods, are equivalent in aggregate to the difference between the historic cost and replacement cost depreciation charges of that period.

(*d*) *Capital gains of current period*

|  | Period | | | | |
| --- | --- | --- | --- | --- | --- |
|  | $t_0-t_1$ £ | $t_1-t_2$ £ | $t_2-t_3$ £ | $t_3-t_4$ £ | Total £ |
| Increase in replacement cost of shop | 1,000(a) | 1,500(b) | 2,500(c) | 300(d) | 5,300 |
| *Less:* realized capital gains of period | — | — | — | 300 | 300 |
| *Unrealized capital gains of current period* | 1,000 | 1,500 | 2,500 | — | 5,000 |

(a) £6,000−5,000; (b) £7,000−6,000; (c) £10,000−7,500; (d) £10,300−10,000.

*Illustration 15d:* Increases in the replacement cost of non-depreciated fixed assets constitute capital gains of a defined period. They can be either unrealized (being increases prior to realization) or realized (being increases accruing solely in the period of realization). Both types of gain constitute part of a current period's business income. (It should be noted that the computation of inventory holding gains is entirely similar in structure and explanation to that accorded to capital gains.)

*(e) Realized capital gains of prior periods*

| | Period | | | | |
|---|---|---|---|---|---|
| | $t_0-t_1$ £ | $t_1-t_2$ £ | $t_2-t_3$ £ | $t_3-t_4$ £ | Total £ |
| Unrealized capital gains of period | 1,000 | 1,500 | 2,500 | — | 5,000 |
| Realized in period $t_3-t_4$ | — | — | — | 5,000 | 5,000 |
| *Realized capital gains of prior periods* | — | — | — | 5,000 | 5,000 |

*Illustration 15e:* As with cost savings and inventory holding gains, unrealized capital gains are realized eventually. When this happens, only that part of the realized gain attributable to the period of realization may be treated as part of the period's business income. The remainder is income of prior periods which, in its unrealized form, will have formed part of prior years' business income. However, despite this, realized capital gains of prior periods are legitimate components of traditional accounting income, because of its reliance on the realization principle, and are included as such.

*(f) Business income of current period*

| | Period | | | | |
|---|---|---|---|---|---|
| | $t_0-t_1$ £ | $t_1-t_2$ £ | $t_2-t_3$ £ | $t_3-t_4$ £ | Total £ |
| Current operating profits[a] | 1,650 | 2,075 | 1,250 | (350) | 4,625 |
| Realized cost savings of period[b] | 50 | 75 | 25 | — | 150 |
| Unrealized cost savings of period[b] | 150 | 150 | 25 | — | 325 |
| Realized capital gains of period[c] | — | — | — | 300 | 300 |
| Unrealized capital gains of period[c] | 1,000 | 1,500 | 2,500 | — | 5,000 |
| *Business income of period* | 2,850 | 3,800 | 3,800 | (50) | 10,400 |

(a) See (15a) above; (b) see (15b) above; (c) see (15d) above.

*Illustration 15f:* This computation follows the framework, already laid down, of current operating profit plus realized and unrealized holding gains accruing in the current period and constituting business income.

**(g)** *Reconciliation of business income and accounting income*

| | Period | | | | |
|---|---|---|---|---|---|
| | $t_0-t_1$ £ | $t_1-t_2$ £ | $t_2-t_3$ £ | $t_3-t_4$ £ | Total £ |
| Business income of period[a] | 2,850 | 3,800 | 3,800 | (50) | 10,400 |
| *Less:* unrealized cost savings of period[b] | 150 | 150 | 25 | — | 325 |
| unrealized capital gains of period[c] | 1,000 | 1,500 | 2,500 | — | 5,000 |
| | 1,150 | 1,650 | 2,525 | — | 5,325 |
| | 1,700 | 2,150 | 1,275 | (50) | 5,075 |
| *Add:* realized cost savings of prior periods[d] | — | 50 | 125 | 150 | 325 |
| realized capital gains of prior periods[e] | — | — | — | 5,000 | 5,000 |
| *Accounting income of period*[f] | 1,700 | 2,200 | 1,400 | 5,100 | 10,400 |

(a) See (15f) above; (b) see (15b) above; (c) see (15d) above; (d) see (15c) above; (e) see (15e) above; (f) see Chapter 4, page 50.

*Illustration 15g:* This section utilizes the aforementioned relationship between business and accounting incomes resulting from the different approaches to the question of realization; i.e. accounting income is derived by subtracting from business income the elements of unrealized holding gains, and adding to it the elements of realized holding gains which have accrued in previous periods.

(*h*) *Financial position on a replacement cost basis*

| | Time | | | | |
|---|---|---|---|---|---|
| | $t_0$ £ | $t_1$ £ | $t_2$ £ | $t_3$ £ | $t_4$ £ |
| Shop | 5,000 | 6,000[a] | 7,500[b] | 10,000[c] | — |
| Van | 1,200 | 1,050[d] | 850[e] | 450[f] | — |
| Cash | — | 2,000[g] | 4,500[h] | 6,200[i] | —[j] |
| *Capital* | 6,200 | 9,050 | 12,850 | 16,650 | — |
| *Increase in capital* | — | 2,850[k] | 3,800[l] | 3,800[m] | (16,650)[n] |

(a) £5,000+1,000; (b) £6,000+1,500; (c) £7,500+2,500; (d) £1,400−$\frac{1}{4}$×£1,400;
(e) £1,700−$\frac{1}{2}$×£1,700; (f) £1,800−$\frac{3}{4}$×£1,800; (g) £0+2,000; (h) £2,000+2,500;
(i) £4,500+1,700; (j) £6,200+10,300+100−16,600; (k) £9,050−6,200;
(l) £12,850−9,050; (m) £16,650−12,850; (n) £0−16,650.

*Illustration 15h:* The purpose of this last section is to demonstrate that business income, measured on a replacement cost basis, can be derived by using a balance sheet approach. Thus, by computing opening and closing accounting capital on a replacement cost basis, business income can be measured as the current value increment over the period concerned – in other words, $Y_b = D+(R_t−R_{t−1})$; where $Y_b$ is the periodic business income; D is the cash distribution to the owner; $R_t$ is the closing capital in replacement cost terms; and $R_{t−1}$ is the opening capital in replacement cost terms; assuming, as throughout the text (see Chapter 1, page 6), that there are no new capital or loan receipts or payments.

The above computations cannot easily reflect the many practical problems related to a business income system of accounting. For example, it has been assumed that replacement costs are known for the resources concerned. It is therefore essential to the measurement of business income for there to be an adequate system of historic cost recording, for it is this data which form the basis to the subsequent current value measurements. In particular, it is important that good records of fixed asset and inventory costs are kept so as to convert the relevant historic costs into contemporary terms for computing cost savings and inventory holding gains. It is also essential that the accounting system be capable of distinguishing between realized and unrealized holding gains, and so, for this reason, it should be capable of producing data which segregate realized resources from those which continue to be held. This is relatively more easily accomplished with fixed assets than with inventory; the number of individual items in the former category are usually far less than in the latter. Parker and Harcourt[10] have suggested a continuous up-dating of historic cost records into replacement cost terms, but the feasibility of this suggestion very much depends on the nature of the business entity and the number of fixed asset and inventory transactions for which it is responsible. Other suggestions to alleviate this practical problem either involve the adjustment of opening and/or closing inventory from a historic cost basis to a replacement cost basis; or a similar adjustment of the cost of sales figure in the traditional accounting income statement from historic cost to a periodic average replacement cost. While these adjustments may have the practical expediency of saving time and costs, besides producing an approximation to current operating profits, they do not necessarily produce credible figures for holding gains or segregate realized from unrealized gains, which objective is a major aim of this particular income model.

## The treatment of holding gains as income

One of the most vexed and little discussed problems arising from the computation of business income is whether holding gains (realized or unrealized) should be classified as income. In a sense, therefore, this problem is similar in outline to the one concerning the treatment of 'windfall' gains as income or capital in the economic model, and, as there, it centres on what capital is required to be maintained.

Edwards and Bell[11] certainly imply that all holding gains accruing in the current period are income, since these form part of their total business income figures. Thus they classify realized and unrealized cost savings, inventory holding gains and capital gains of the period concerned as income. To the extent (as demonstrated in Illustration 15, Section 15h), that they represent an increase in the money value aggregate of replacement cost capital, this particular treatment may seem to be appropriate. Prakash and Sunder[12] have also recently argued that, because (a) operating and holding decisions are not independent; (b) current operating profit is no better a predictor than business income; and (c) business owners are only interested in changes in money wealth, the separation of operating and holding gains is an arbitrary and unattractive dichotomy. It should, however, also be stated that this is not the only way in which replacement cost capital maintenance may be perceived. Capital can be determined as an aggregation of physical resources expressed in money terms; and also by the more simple approach of an aggregate money total. If capital is thought of in terms of physical resources, and therefore in terms of operating capacity, this alters the argument for treating holding gains as income and, instead, for treating current operating profit only as income.

First, although unrealized holding gains represent a change in the money value attributed to resources, they do not represent any change in the amount of physical resources available to the entity. Secondly, realized holding gains need not necessarily represent any change in available physical resources if the cash realized has to be utilized to replace the realized resources concerned at a cost different from the original cost. Only when the realized resource is not replaced can there be said to be a realized holding gain representing a physical change in existing resources. Even in these cases, the cash may be utilized to acquire equivalent resources to maintain an entity's operating capacity. Thus the treatment of the realized holding gains as income becomes a somewhat dubious procedure, as the following example may help to clarify. (Part of Illustration 15 is again used.)

Assume at $t_0$ that a shop is purchased for £5,000. Its replacement cost changes as follows: at $t_1$, £6,000; at $t_2$, £7,500; and at $t_3$, £10,000. Soon after $t_3$, the shop is sold for £10,300.

From these figures, the following points emerge: (1) expressed in monetary terms, capital amounts to £5,000 at $t_0$, £6,000 at $t_1$, £7,500 at $t_2$, £10,000 at $t_3$, and £10,300 after $t_3$. (2) This evidently reveals unrealized value increments of £1,000 for the period $t_0-t_1$, £1,500 for the period $t_1-t_2$, £2,500 for the period $t_2-t_3$, and a realized value increment of £300 for the period $t_3-t_4$. (3) After sale, monetary resources have thus increased by a total of £5,300 over the entire period, and, in this sense, such a figure could be regarded as income. (4) However, prior to the sale, although the current value of the shop increased in each period, such value increments did not create an equivalent increase in physical resources – the only available resource being the shop. (5) Therefore these unrealized gains do not appear to represent anything other than a readjustment of the various opening values for capital – i.e. capital maintenance adjustments. (6) Once the shop has been sold, and the entire holding gain of £5,300 realized, the owner of capital is £5,300 better off in money terms than he was before he bought the shop. (7) To the extent that he reinvests this gain in another property, he is no better off in terms of physical resources and only the portion of the gain not reinvested could be deemed to be

income. (8) However, in the majority of instances, when holding gains
are earned and eventually realized by an entity with a long-term life,
these gains are normally reinvested so as to maintain the physical
operating capacity of the business, and, because of this, they should not
be treated as income.

To achieve an adequate maintenance of capital in terms of physical
operating capacity, it is evident from the above comments that all
holding gains ought to be treated as capital maintenance adjustments,
and that current operating profits should not contain holding gains.
Within this context, the identification of holding gains on non-
depreciating assets (such as the shop in Illustration 15) is relatively
straightforward. However, the situation with depreciable assets (such
as the motor van) is more complex.

The general principle to be applied to the van is that the replacement
cost adjustments should allow for the maintenance of capital in
physical resource terms (and thus for the replacement of the van at its
current gross replacement cost). In order to do this, at any particular
date, the replacement cost depreciation deductions from income
should, together with the current potential sale proceeds of the van,
provide for this sum. In Illustration 15, this is not the case because of
the underprovision of depreciation in previous periods.

Taking the depreciation figures in Illustration 15 (a), the total
amount written off in arriving at current operating profits is £1,575.
This, together with the sale value just after $t_3$ of £100, provides total
funds of £1,675 to meet a potential replacement cost at the same date
of £1,800. The shortfall is £125, representing the 'backlog' depreciation described in Illustration 15 (b) (£75 in period $t_1$–$t_2$ and £50 in
period $t_2$–$t_3$) which has not been charged against income, being
deducted instead from the unrealized holding gains on the van. Thus,
in order to maintain physical operating capacity, it is necessary to make
further capital maintenance adjustments when determining the level
of distribution – that is, by deducting £75 (at $t_2$) and £50 (at $t_3$) from
aggregate current operating profits (these sums would be added to the
cumulative totals of holding gains being treated as capital adjustments). However, as this text is concerned with the measurement of
income and capital, and not with particular situations in which these
measurements could be applied, these further capital maintenance
adjustments have not been made in the relevant illustrations.

What this brief commentary on the nature of holding gains implies is
that current operating profits are the only elements of business income
which positively add to the physical resources and operating capacity
of the entity, and, if this is how the concept of capital maintenance is to

be applied in this current value model, then holding gains should be treated as capital maintenance adjustments and not as income. On the other hand, if capital maintenance is viewed solely in money terms, then such gains could be classified as income. Everything therefore depends on the perception of capital and its maintenance.

## Advantages and disadvantages of replacement cost

The final section of the present chapter deals with the various merits and demerits of an income determination process based on current replacement costs.

The first advantage of the system is its concentration (by exclusion of holding gains from business income) on maintenance of physical rather than monetary resources. In other words, by emphasizing current operating profits, it segregates elements of gain which need not necessarily mean an increase in the operating capacity of the business entity concerned. Thus it tends to aid management in its decision making in relation to dividend and retention policies – particularly if holding gains are treated as capital maintenance adjustments. It must be emphasized, however, that this is an advantage of the current operating profit variant of business income rather than of the concept of business income devised by Edwards and Bell.

Secondly, by separating operational from holding gains, the business income model distinguishes gains thought to be more within the control of management from those which may not be entirely within its control. This may help investors and others to assess the effectiveness of management in conducting entity affairs; and also may aid management in the process of self-assessment. However, it is only fair to state that this is a somewhat dubious point to argue. Operating and holding decisions in business are inevitably and necessarily interdependent, and thus the value of interpreting data implying the independence of these matters ought to be treated with some care (and at least within the context of the circumstances of the business concerned).

The third advantage of the system is its recognition of current values, and its abandonment of the realization principle and the conservatism convention: factors which render the resulting accounting information more relevant and useful to an individual concerned with assessing the progress and present situation of an entity he is involved or interested in. The concept of business income thus eliminates many of the faults of the traditional accounting model – e.g. the latter's misleading view of values in the balance sheet, and its incomprehensible heterogeneous mixture of gains in the aggregate income figure.

The fourth major advantage of the system is its feasibility, both in terms of time and cost. One of the major arguments put up against the replacement cost system is that it may be far too costly and time-consuming to be of much advantage over and above the existing system of measuring accounting income. However, as Dickerson[13] has demonstrated, time and cost are not significant constraining factors to the implementation of a business income concept.

There are, however, a number of significant disadvantages to the replacement cost system, and these need to be mentioned. First, unless there is an adequate historic cost system available for use as a foundation to replacement costs, the credibility of business income measures must remain open to some doubt. Therefore replacement cost does not mean the complete abandonment of historic cost. Secondly, although the business income concept is based on current values, it only utilizes values for resources which are accounted for through the traditional historic cost system. Thus, many intangible resources, of undoubted value to particular entities, are not accounted for because they have not been the subject of historic cost transactions. Thirdly, there is the question of whether the replacement costs should be those relevant to resources identical with or equivalent to those at present held for use or resale. This is a problem which involves replacement policy, obsolescence and technical change. It is also a problem of finding appropriate and credible replacement costs for individual resources, for such figures are not always readily available or computable because of the nature of the resources concerned (an example of such resources would be highly specialized and custom built machinery). In other words, a particular resource may not be replaced in the future or a resource may be replaced by an equivalent one rather than an identical one. Some might argue for identical resources and others for equivalent ones. In addition, some might argue for the use of replacement costs of new assets, adjusted for depreciation, and others for replacement costs of used assets of similar condition to existing ones. The problem, therefore, is that different replacement costs for the same asset will produce different business income figures and thereby increase the potential flexibility in financial accounting practice.

Whether these are serious problems is now at least open to some doubt. First, Revsine[14] has recently argued at length to demonstrate that, in terms of simple operating returns on capital (expressed in replacement cost terms), it does not matter whether replacement costs of 'old technology' or 'new technology' assets are used (similar returns being achieved); and that the only problem is the need to consider the difficulties associated with using 'new technology' replacement costs and adopting them to the 'old technology' assets. Secondly, the use of second-hand replacement costs avoids the problems of cost allocation in the depreciation process (and also of so-called 'backlog' depreciation) but hardly appears to conform with the verity criterion – in other words, few businesses would replace a used asset with a similar used asset.

The final major disadvantage of the system is that it cannot be regarded as having universal application and relevance in the business world. Some businesses are fixed asset and inventory intensive, and may hold these resources for some considerable time prior to realization. In these instances, the business income concept (and its current operating profit variant) would seem to be most appropriate. However, in businesses having few fixed assets and a high turnover of inventory, it appears far less useful because most of the elements of gain will be of an operational nature. In other words, these would be situations where historic cost and replacement cost approximate. Holding gains would, nevertheless, still exist, being accumulated as a result of the high turnover of resources.

## References

(See page 178 for Selected Bibliography)

1. E. O. Edwards and P. W. Bell, *The Theory and Measurement of Business Income*, University of California Press, 1961.

2. American Accounting Association, *A Statement of Basic Accounting Theory*, 1966.

3. R. T. Sprouse and M. Moonitz, 'A Tentative Set of Broad Accounting Principles for Business Enterprises', *Accounting Research Study 3*, American Institute of Certified Public Accountants, 1962.

4. L. Revsine, *Replacement Cost Accounting*, Prentice-Hall, 1973.

5. As argued in P. Prakash and S. Sunder, 'The Case Against Separation of Current Operating Profit and Holding Gain', *Accounting Review*, January 1979, pp. 1–22.

6. Edwards and Bell, *The Theory and Measurement of Business Income*, p. 79.

7. K. P. Gee and K. V. Peasnell, 'A Pragmatic Defence of Replacement Cost', *Accounting and Business Research*, Autumn 1976, pp. 242–9.

8. Edwards and Bell, *The Theory and Measurement of Business Income*.

9. For example, Parker and Harcourt, op. cit., pp. 4–7.

10. ibid., pp. 20–25.

11. Edwards and Bell, op. cit., passim.

12. Prakash and Sunder, op. cit.

13. P. J. Dickerson, *Business Income – A Critical Analysis*, Institute of Business and Economic Research, University of California, 1965.

14. Revsine, op. cit.

# 7 Current exit values and realizable income

## The case for exit values

The alternative to entry prices, in the current value income model, is exit prices or realizable market values. This particular model was first advocated by MacNeal[1] in the 1930s, and has since been developed by Chambers[2] and Sterling.[3] It may be identified as $Y_r = D + (R_t - R_{t-1})$; where $Y_r$ is the realizable income; D is the periodic distribution of income; $R_t$ is the closing capital valued on an exit price basis; and $R_{t-1}$ is the opening capital valued on the same basis; assuming no new capital or loan receipts or repayments. Thus, the concept of realizable income is concerned with the periodic change in the realizable value of transactions-based capital. The use of selling prices, however, raises one important issue: what selling price should be used, for various alternatives are available? Should they be those arising from an assumed liquidation of the entire entity (as in bankruptcy), or should they be based on the assumption of orderly liquidation (as in the normal course of business events)? Should they be the realizable values of the resources in their existing state, or should they be potential realizations of the resources in their finished state, but adjusted for future costs? These questions have been raised at various times with regard to realizable income, and it is generally agreed among its advocates that the realizable values used should be (a) those assuming orderly rather than forced resource realizations; and (b) based on market prices existing at the time of measurement and reporting rather than adjusted future selling prices.

The realizable income model is based on the well-known economic concept of opportunity cost – i.e. value expressed in terms of what the owner of resources is sacrificing by having them in their existing form rather than in a next best alternative form. The alternative opportunity costs are either value in terms of the cash to be derived from a realization of the resources, or value in terms of the present discounted value of benefits which could be derived from investing the realized cash in the form of alternative non-cash resources. But since the problem of determining the latter concept of value is so fraught with difficulties, and so open-ended, net realizable value is usually advocated as the most reasonable opportunity cost to use. It is an expression of the economic sacrifice being made by the entity when it invests in the resources it has rather than in alternatives. Such a sacrifice is therefore expressed in terms of the entity's ability to command alternative goods and services – i.e. what it could acquire with the cash it would have if it realized its existing resources.

Not many accountants or economists support this particular income model, mainly because it implies liquidation rather than continuity of the business entity. However, the following are the arguments which have been put forward in support of its use:

1 *Realizable values are measures of current sacrifices and alternative choices.* This particular argument states the view that managers, owners and other persons interested in the affairs of a business entity should receive accounting information which reflects the economic sacrifices being made by the entity when holding resources in their existing form. Realizable values reflect the alternative resource form; i.e. what the entity would have in the form of cash if its existing resources were realized in an orderly manner. This information is regarded by the advocates of the realizable income model as useful and relevant to a whole range of interested persons because it underlies a vital economic decision of importance to them all: should the entity continue in its existing form or would it be better off in an alternative form? Realizable values portray the basis to that alternative.

2 *Entry values are invalid.* The supporters of realizable income state that exit values are more appropriate than entry values because the latter do not reflect alternatives or choice, factors which are fundamental to economic position, once the decision to hold and use resources in their existing form has been made. Replacement cost therefore does not inform the decision maker of the economic sacrifice being made by holding entity resources in their existing form. Also, as Sterling[4] has pointed out, the entry value model of business income is based on the invalid and unnecessary assumption of the entity as a going concern with an indefinite life. Exit values ignore this assumption, and, in fact, rely on the counter-assumption that the entity will have only a definite life in its existing form.

*3 Comparable data are required.* One of the most important factors in information processing is to ensure that the information user is supplied with comparable data for assessing alternatives and making decisions. If the data for a particular entity are in entry value terms, then they reflect the cost of replacement for that entity only. Thus values may be completely different for a comparable entity which has a different resource structure. It is therefore argued by the advocates of exit values that these bring greater comparability of data from similar entities because the values are expressed in terms relevant to most businesses: the ability of cash to command other goods and services.

*4 Understandability.* A great deal of the argument for exit values is centred around this point, that realizable values are values which most people understand best and can identify with. In other words, realizable values are commonly interpreted as market values. Whereas it is somewhat difficult to explain current value in terms of replacement costs, it is much easier to explain realizable values.

*5 Evidence of use of realizable values.* Chambers[5] has put forward a very persuasive argument for exit values in income determination by giving examples of situations in current accounting practice where the use of realizable values is advocated and practised. He does this to show that the realizable income model is a logical extension of these practices, and cites the following examples: (a) the valuation of net monetary assets at exit values; (b) the 'lower of cost or market' rule for inventory valuation; (c) the U.K. legal disclosure requirements regarding the market values of land, buildings and investments; and (d) the occasional revaluation of certain fixed assets, such as land and buildings.

## The concept of realizable income

As we have seen, realizable income is a measure of the periodic change in the capital of an entity when this is measured in exit value terms. It consists of two main components: realized and unrealized gains of the period; realized gains representing the difference between the realized value and the previously computed realizable value (or the acquisition value, if the resource concerned was acquired during the period of realization) and unrealized gains representing the difference between the realizable values of the resource concerned at beginning and end of the period (or between acquisition cost and the end of period realizable value, if it was acquired during the period). Thus $Y_r = RG + UG$; where $Y_r$ is the realizable income of the period; RG are the realized exit value gains of the current period; and UG are the unrealized exit value gains of the current period. In addition, the realized gains of the period can be analysed between operating gains resulting from trading activities involving resources previously held for resale, and non-operating gains resulting from the sale of resources previously held for use. The unrealized gains can similarly be segregated according to the type of resource concerned.

The concept of realizable income is shown in the following simple example:

Assume 1,000 units of inventory were purchased at $t_0$ for £1,000. At $t_1$ their realizable value was £1,300, and at $t_2$ their realizable value was £2,000 (at which point they were sold). During the period $t_0 - t_1$, realizable income would be £1,300 − 1,000 = £300 (an unrealized operational gain; inventory being held specifically for resale). In the period $t_1 - t_2$, realizable income would be £2,000 − 1,300 = £700 (a realized operational gain).

In contrast to this approach, traditional accounting income would recognize no income in period $t_0 - t_1$ (as none had been realized) and £1,000 of income in period $t_1 - t_2$ (£2,000 minus the original acquisition cost of £1,000). The difference, therefore, between realizable income and accounting income is one of realization (as was the difference between accounting and business incomes). Realizable income recognizes unrealized value changes in the period they arise, and consequently does not include realized gains of previous periods in its computations – as is the case with accounting income. In other words, when $Y_r = RG + UG$ (as defined above) and $Y_a = RG + RG'$ where $Y_a$ is the accounting income of the period; RG are the realized exit value gains of the current period (operational and non-operational); and RG' are the realized exit value gains of the current period accrued in previous periods (again, operational and non-operational); then $Y_r - UG + RG' = Y_a$.

## Realizable income in practice

Illustration 16, which utilizes the basic figures already used in Chapters 4 and 6, describes the process of measuring realizable income in accordance with the concepts described briefly in the preceding section. They loosely adhere to the format designed by Chambers,[6] in which unrealized changes in the exit values of depreciable assets are described as depreciation; and all other unrealized exit value changes are described as price variations. (It should be noted that the capital maintenance adjustments advocated by Chambers have been omitted at this point in the text. They will be discussed in Chapter 10.)

A business opened at $t_0$ with the purchase of a motor van for £1,200 and a shop for £5,000; cash operating surpluses before depreciation were £2,000 for the period $t_0-t_1$, £2,500 for the period $t_1-t_2$, and £1,700 for the period $t_2-t_3$. Business operations ceased immediately after $t_3$ when the van was sold for £100 and the shop for £10,300. Depreciation of the van, for traditional accounting purposes, was written off over four years on a straight-line basis with estimated nil sale proceeds. In addition, the following net realizable values were relevant to the van and the shop at the stated dates; at $t_1$, van £850, shop £5,700; at $t_2$, van £350, shop £7,000; and at $t_3$, van £100, shop £9,500.

The following comments explain the computations in the illustration:

*Illustration 16a*: In each period the measure of realizable income is composed of various realized and unrealized operating and non-operating gains. The realized operational surplus is adjusted by the unrealized realizable value changes (increases and decreases) relevant

**Illustration 16  Computation of realizable income**
*(a) Realizable income*

|                          | Period |        |        |        |        |
|--------------------------|--------|--------|--------|--------|--------|
|                          | $t_0-t_1$ £ | $t_1-t_2$ £ | $t_2-t_3$ £ | $t_3-t_4$ £ | Total £ |
| Operating gain of period | 2,000  | 2,500  | 1,700  | —      | 6,200  |
| *Less*: depreciation of van | 350[(a)] | 500[(b)] | 250[(c)] | —   | 1,100  |
|                          | 1,650  | 2,000  | 1,450  | —      | 5,100  |
| *Add*: price variations on shop: |  |    |        |        |        |
| unrealized               | 700[(d)] | 1,300[(e)] | 2,500[(f)] | — | 4,500 |
| realized                 | —      | —      | —      | 800[(g)] | 800   |
| *Realizable income of period* | 2,350 | 3,300 | 3,950 | 800  | 10,400 |

(a) £1,200−850; (b) £850−350; (c) £350−100; (d) £5,700−5,000; (e) £7,000−5,700; (f) £9,500−7,000; (g) £10,300−9,500.

*(b) Reconciliation of realizable income and accounting income*

|  | Period | | | | |
| --- | --- | --- | --- | --- | --- |
|  | $t_0-t_1$ £ | $t_1-t_2$ £ | $t_2-t_3$ £ | $t_3-t_4$ £ | Total £ |
| Realizable income of period | 2,350 | 3,300 | 3,950 | 800 | 10,400 |
| *Less*: depreciation differences | (50)[a] | (200)[b] | 50[c] | 200[d] | — |
|  | 2,400 | 3,500 | 3,900 | 600 | 10,400 |
| *Less*: price variation differences | 700 [e] | 1,300 [f] | 2,500[g] | (4,500)[h] | — |
| *Accounting income of period* | 1,700 | 2,200 | 1,400 | 5,100 | 10,400 |

(a) £300−350; (b) £300−500; (c) £300−250; (d) £200−0; (e) £700−0; (f) £1,300−0; (g) £2,500−0; (h) £0−(£700+1,300+2,500).

*(c) Financial position on a realizable value basis*

|  | Time | | | | |
| --- | --- | --- | --- | --- | --- |
|  | $t_0$ £ | $t_1$ £ | $t_2$ £ | $t_3$ £ | $t_4$ £ |
| Shop | 5,000 | 5,700[a] | 7,000[b] | 9,500[c] | — |
| Van | 1,200 | 850[d] | 350[e] | 100[f] | — |
| Cash | — | 2,000[g] | 4,500[h] | 6,200[i] | —[j] |
| *Capital* | 6,200 | 8,550 | 11,850 | 15,800 | — |
| *Increase in capital* | — | 2,350[k] | 3,300[l] | 3,950[m] | (15,800)[n] |

(a) £5,000+700; (b) £5,700+1,300; (c) £7,000+2,500; (d) £1,200−350; (e) £850−500; (f) £350−250; (g) £0+2,000; (h) £2,000+2,500; (i) £4,500+1,700; (j) £6,200+100+10,300−16,600; (k) £8,550−6,200; (l) £11,850−8,550; (m) £15,800−11,850; (n) £0−15,800.

to the van and shop in each of the first three periods. In the period of final entity realization, there being no unrealized gains or operating surplus, the only income element is the realized gain on the shop accruing in that period. The overall result of each period's computations is that the periodic income aggregate, and thus each of its elements, is accrued and earned during that period. Therefore each income figure conforms properly with the so-called verity criterion – i.e. it conforms with economic reality by reflecting the overall increase (or decrease) in the entity's generalized capacity to command goods and services.

*Illustration 16b*: The reconciliation reveals that traditional accounting measures can be derived from realizable income measures, and vice versa, by adjusting for (a) unrealized price changes not accounted for in the traditional model; and (b) prior period price changes already accounted for in the realizable model as unrealized price changes when they were accruing.

*Illustration 16c*: This remaining section is given to demonstrate that realizable income, as with all the other income models described in this text, can be derived from a comparison of opening and closing periodic capital, after making allowance for the final distribution to the owner.

## Business income and realizable income

It has been emphasized, both in this and the preceding chapter, that the concepts of business and realizable incomes abandon the traditional accounting principle of realization, and thereby incorporate unrealized gains of each period and avoid heterogeneous mixtures of current and prior period gains. However, although both concepts contain these similar elements, they are each based upon differing values: business income uses entry values or replacement costs, and realizable income uses exit values or net realizable values. The essential difference, therefore, between the concepts is the periodic difference between the entry value and the exit value of each resource held by the entity. Following the general principle that an entity will normally hold a non-monetary resource as long as its replacement cost is higher than its net realizable value (and assuming its economic value is, at least, in excess of the latter value, and that prices are increasing over time), then, prior to its realization, the resource's entry value will usually exceed its exit value, and the replacement cost model will incorporate aggregate unrealized values changes in excess of the corresponding total in the net realizable value model. However, when the resource is realized, a realized exit value change in excess of the corresponding entry value change will result. This difference is equivalent to the excess of unrealized entry value changes in previous years. Thus, the relationship between business income and realizable income can be identified as follows: $Y_b - UV + RV' = Y_r$; where $Y_b$ is the business income of the period; UV are the unrealized value differences of the current period representing the periodic change in the excess of total entry values over total exit values; RV' are the realized value differences of the current period, accruing in previous periods, and representing the previous unrealized entry value excesses now converted into exit values by realization; and $Y_r$ is the realizable income of the period. This relationship can best be followed by taking the worked example used in the present chapter in connection with realizable income, and in Chapter 6 in connection with business income. Taking the financial positions outlined in each previous illustration as a basis, Illustration 17 analyses the difference between business and realizable incomes.

**Illustration 17   Relationship between business and realizable incomes**
*(a) Financial position on a replacement cost basis*[a]

|  | Time | | | | |
|---|---|---|---|---|---|
|  | $t_0$ £ | $t_1$ £ | $t_2$ £ | $t_3$ £ | $t_4$ £ |
| Shop | 5,000 | 6,000 | 7,500 | 10,000 | — |
| Van | 1,200 | 1,050 | 850 | 450 | — |
| Cash | — | 2,000 | 4,500 | 6,200 | — |
| *Capital* | 6,200 | 9,050 | 12,850 | 16,650 | — |
| *Business income* | — | 2,850 | 3,800 | 3,800 | (50) |

(a) As per Illustration 15.

*(b) Financial position on a realizable value basis*[a]

|  | Time | | | | |
|---|---|---|---|---|---|
|  | $t_0$ £ | $t_1$ £ | $t_2$ £ | $t_3$ £ | $t_4$ £ |
| Shop | 5,000 | 5,700 | 7,000 | 9,500 | — |
| Van | 1,200 | 850 | 350 | 100 | — |
| Cash | — | 2,000 | 4,500 | 6,200 | — |
| *Capital* | 6,200 | 8,550 | 11,850 | 15,800 | — |
| *Realizable income* | — | 2,350 | 3,300 | 3,950 | 800 |

(a) As per Illustration 16.

*(c) Reconciliation of business and realizable incomes*

| | Period | | | | |
|---|---|---|---|---|---|
| | $t_0-t_1$ £ | $t_1-t_2$ £ | $t_2-t_3$ £ | $t_3-t_4$ £ | Total £ |
| Business income (as above) | 2,850 | 3,800 | 3,800 | (50) | 10,400 |
| *Less*: unrealized excess entry value changes: | | | | | |
| van | 200 (a) | 300 (b) | (150) (c) | — | 350 |
| shop | 300 (d) | 200 (e) | — (f) | — | 500 |
| | 500 | 500 | (150) | — | 850 |
| | 2,350 | 3,300 | 3,950 | (50) | 9,550 |
| *Add*: realized excess entry value changes of previous periods: | | | | | |
| van | — | — | — | 350(g) | 350 |
| shop | — | — | — | 500(h) | 500 |
| *Realizable income* (as above) | 2,350 | 3,300 | 3,950 | 800 | 10,400 |

(a) £1,050−850; (b) (£850−350)−£200; (c) (£450−100)−(£200+300);
(d) £6,000−5,700; (e) (£7,500−7,000)−£300; (f) (£10,000−9,500)−(£300+200);
(g) (£450−100)−(£100−100); (h) (£10,000−10,300)−(£9,500−10,300).

This reconciliation reveals the previously mentioned conceptual relationship between the two current value income concepts. By comparing the corresponding balance sheet values for each resource, the realized and unrealized value and gain differences can be determined – e.g. at $t_1$, the van has an entry value of £1,050 compared with an exit value of £850; this means that an unrealized entry value difference of £200 has been included in business income. At $t_2$, the difference has widened to £500, of which £300 refers to the current period; and at $t_3$, it is down to £350, which means that a 'negative' unrealized entry value difference of £150 has occurred in that period. When the van is sold, there is a £350 loss in entry value terms compared with a nil gain in exit value terms – the difference between the two representing the realization of the previously accrued unreal-

*(d) Realizable values and asset replacement*

| | Time | | | |
|---|---|---|---|---|
| | $t_1$ £ | $t_2$ £ | $t_3$ £ | $t_{3+}$ [a] £ |
| Net realizable values of [b]: | | | | |
| van | 850 | 350 | 100 | 100 |
| shop | 5,700 | 7,000 | 9,500 | 10,300 |
| | 6,550 | 7,350 | 9,600 | 10,400 |
| *Add*: aggregate net realizable value depreciation on van | 350[c] | 850[d] | 1,100[e] | 1,100[f] |
| | 6,900 | 8,200 | 10,700 | 11,500 |
| *Less*: replacement cost of [g]: | | | | |
| van | 1,400 | 1,700 | 1,800 | 1,800 |
| shop | 6,000 | 7,500 | 10,000 | 10,000 |
| | 7,400 | 9,200 | 11,800 | 11,800 |
| *Additional finance requirement* | 500 | 1,000 | 1,100 | 300 |
| of which explained by: (i) gap between entry and exit values in balance sheet: | | | | |
| van | 200[h] | 500[i] | 350[j] | —[k] |
| shop | 300[l] | 500[m] | 500[n] | (300)[o] |
| | 500 | 1,000 | 850 | (300) |
| (ii) differences between entry and exit value depreciation aggregate provisions: | | | | |
| van | —[p] | —[q] | 250[r] | 600[s] |
| | 500 | 1,000 | 1,100 | 300 |

(a) Assumed to be immediately following $t_3$; (b) as given in Illustration 16; (c) £1,200−850; (d) £350+(£850−350); (e) £850+(£350−100); (f) as in (e); (g) as given in Illustration 15; (h) £1,050−850; (i) £850  350; (j) £450−100; (k) £100−100; (l) £6,000−5,700; (m) £7,500−7,000; (n) £10,000−9,500; (o) £10,000−10,300; (p) £350−350; (q) (£350+500)−(£350+500); (r) (£850+500)−(£850+250); (s) (£1,350+350)−£1,100.

ized valuation differences of £200 ($t_0-t_1$), £300 ($t_1-t_2$) and £(150) ($t_2-t_3$). The reader may follow a similar computational pattern with the shop.

These differences also partly explain the additional finance that would require to be raised if the entity were accounted for on an exit value basis, and the shop and the van were replaced (i.e., if continuity was assumed). This is demonstrated in (d) below. All the figures have been introduced in relevant parts of this and the preceding chapter.

The above figures reveal that, at least in this case, the exit value model fails to provide sufficient funds (in terms of sale values and depreciation provisions) to replace the two assets concerned (should that be required). In fact, at the point at which the shop and van are realized ($t_{3+}$), the shortfall in funds is £300, of which £600 is due to inadequate provision of exit value depreciation on the van – £1,200 being available instead of the £1,800 needed to replace it at that time, and £(300) being the surplus funds available from the sale of the shop (for £10,300) to replace it if required (at £10,000). The reconciliation figures at $t_1$, $t_2$ and $t_3$ reflect the accumulation of this position in terms of the gaps between entry and exit values, and the underprovision of exit value depreciation.

The above paragraphs have attempted to describe the quantitative relationship between the business and realizable income models. The remainder of this section is devoted to an explanation of the conceptual differences between the two. They are, too often, regarded as competing rather than complementary alternatives in income determination. For example, Edwards and Bell[7] did not favour the concept of realizable income because it does not assume indefinite continuity of business activity. On the other hand, Sterling[8] rejected business income because it does not reflect alternatives and sacrifices.

The replacement cost model of business income is founded on the idea of maintaining capital in terms of money and, in the case of current operating profit, in terms of either identical or equivalent physical goods and services, whereas the net realizable model of realizable income maintains capital in terms of its generalized command over goods and services. Therefore, each utilizes different value and capital maintenance concepts. This suggests that each may have an entirely separate role to play, depending on the particular use to which the relevant information has to be put. Each concept has features essential to decision making, since both are expressed in the contemporary terms needed by a decision maker concerned with making a decision on the basis of a present business situation. The current operating profit variant of the business income model, for example, seems most relevant to decisions which assume the continuity of the business entity, replacement of its existing resources and long-term survival. The realizable income model, on the other hand, seems most relevant when decisions about alternative investments or entity forms are being considered. As the questions of survival and continuity of the business entity are central to both types of decision, it is fair to assume that each concept will be useful to decision makers who wish meaningfully to analyse and consider these separate questions. Certainly, each appears to be entirely relevant to the internal management of a business entity, as well as to those persons and bodies who have or are about to invest in it. These are all concerned with the benefits to be derived from keeping the entity in its present form or reinvesting in an alternative form. It would therefore seem appropriate to report both types of income and value measures so as to provide managers, investors and others with all the relevant and necessary information. This follows the philosophy, to be developed later in this book, of different income and value measures for differing decision and control purposes. It also follows the view that multi-purpose information and reports could well be more useful and relevant to information users as a whole (because each particular type of information is tailor-made to particular purposes) than is general purpose information (which, because of its general nature, is not entirely useful or relevant to anyone).

### Holding gains as realizable income

The concept of realizable income includes non-operational or non-trading gains and losses (price variations) which are rather similar to the holding gains which arose in the business income model; again assuming, as through earlier chapters, a constant value for money. The question then arises as to whether or not these unrealized and realized gains should be treated as income. The answer is certainly not as complex as it is with business income. Capital in the realizable income model is an expression of the entity's overall command over goods and services in general, and any increase in this expression of wealth could properly be described as income; the reason being that it is not the intention of this model to maintain capital in physical operating capacity terms. Therefore, if the potential realizable proceeds of an entity's existing resources has increased over a period, it has, potentially, more available to invest in alternative forms, and thus it has increased its wealth. Income may therefore be said to exist because, if the value increment was consumed by way of dividend, capital in terms of command over goods and services would still be maintained.

## The case against realizable income

It is only fair to summarize some of the major criticisms which have been levelled at the realizable income model. The first is that it concentrates primarily on the overall change in realizable value during a period, and does not pay much attention to the operational effectiveness of the entity – as is the case with business income and its main element of current operating profit. Indeed, it has even been suggested that the use of realizable values is a total abandonment of income measurement.[9] From this it is said to follow that realizable income does not differentiate between those gains within the control of management and those outside such control. This criticism is not, however, particularly valid, for, as we saw in Illustration 16, it is possible to segregate operational and non-operational gains. In any case, there is arguable doubt as to the need to segregate such gains because of their interdependence.[10] Also, there is no evidence to suggest that current operating profits are any more controllable (and therefore predictable) than either replacement cost holding gains, realizable value operating gains, or price variations.

Possibly the weightiest argument against the realizable income concept is its apparent assumption of liquidation of entity resources, or, indeed, of the entity itself. The concept is said to ignore the counter-assumption of continuity of business activity indefinitely. However, while liquidation is implied in the concept, it is argued by its advocates that this need not mean it is contemplated. Indeed, the main purpose of using the realizable income model is to inform managers, investors and other interested parties of the existence of alternative courses of action open to the entity, no matter how unpleasant the implications of these alternatives may be.

The last major criticism of realizable income is one made on practical rather than conceptual grounds. It concerns the difficulty of determining realizable values for particular entity resources, many of which may have no known marketable value (e.g. intangibles such as goodwill, or tangibles such as plant and machinery) or which may take a form not presently saleable (e.g. as in the case of semi-processed inventory). This complaint can be exaggerated, however, as realizable values are either known or can be imputed, as McKeown[11] proved in a recent case study.

## References

(See page 178–9 for Selected Bibliography)

1. K. MacNeal, *Truth in Accounting*, Scholars Book Co., 1970 (reprint).

2. R. J. Chambers, *Accounting, Evaluation and Economic Behaviour*, Prentice-Hall. 1966.

3. R. R. Sterling, *Theory of the Measurement of Enterprise Income*, University of Kansas Press, 1970.

4. R. R. Sterling, 'The Going Concern: An Examination', *Accounting Review*, July 1968, pp. 481–502.

5. R. J. Chambers, 'Evidence for a Market – Selling Price – Accounting System', in R. R. Sterling (ed.), *Asset Valuation and Income Determination – a Consideration of Alternatives*, Scholars Book Co., 1971, pp. 74–96.

6. As described in R. J. Chambers, 'Accounting for Inflation', *Exposure Draft*, University of Sydney, 1975.

7. E. O. Edwards and P. W. Bell, *The Theory and Measurement of Business Income*, University of California Press, 1961, p. 275.

8. Sterling, *Theory of the Measurement of Enterprise Income*, pp. 328–9.

9. A. L. Thomas, 'The Allocation Problem in Financial Accounting Theory', *Studies in Accounting Research 3*, American Accounting Association, 1969, p. 104.

10. P. Prakash and S. Sunder, 'The Case Against Separation of Current Operating Profit and Holding Gain', *Accounting Review*, January 1979, pp. 1–22.

11. J. C. McKeown, 'An Empirical Test of a Model Proposed by Chambers', *Accounting Review*, January 1971, pp. 12–29.

# 8 Mixed values and current cost income

## Introduction

In Chapters 6 and 7 we have attempted to describe the two main current value models – business income which utilizes entry prices, and realizable income which utilizes exit prices. As such, and allowing for the necessary use of exit prices for liquid and near-liquid assets in the business income model, both measures of income can be said to rely on a single valuation basis. However, in relatively recent times, a third current value school of thought has emerged – i.e. the current cost income school which bases its measurement of periodic income on the concept of value to the business. Its support is such that it is to be evidenced in professional accounting pronouncements issued in various countries, as well as in numerous parts of the academic literature. The purpose of this chapter is to explain these developments within the theoretical framework used throughout this text. Hopefully, this will provide the reader with a necessary introduction to significant changes in accounting practice.

*Ad hoc* arguments for mixed value approaches to the determination of income and capital are not unusual. MacNeal,[1] for example, suggested that replacement costs should be used in the realizable income when realizable values are not available for particular assets. Sprouse and Moonitz[2] utilized several valuation bases, dependent on the type of asset concerned. Ross[3] and Arthur Andersen and Co.[4] have argued independently that, when measuring current value income, a mixture of replacement costs and realizable values should be used where appropriate. Grinyer and Lewis[5] have advocated the use of net realizable values for fixed assets, and replacement costs for current assets. The idea of a mixed value model has been applied in practice in a number of countries – occasionally in the form of a full set of financial statements and, alternatively, by way of supplementary notes to the historic cost statements. Whatever the disclosure method, the primary purpose is usually the measurement of current cost income, and the basis of accounting is the concept of value to the business – the maximum loss the reporting entity would suffer should it be deprived of the assets it holds. As such, it has been adapted from its original legal context provided by Bonbright[6] (dealing with judicial reparation for lost property). For its growing use within the practice of financial reporting, value to the business owes much to writers such as Wright,[7] Solomons,[8] Stamp,[9] and Baxter.[10] Each has aided its explanation and definition, and ensured its adaptation to the context of business. However, in the process of development, the concept has been variously described as value to the owner, deprival value, and value to the business. It is the latter term which will be used throughout the remainder of this chapter.

## The case for mixed values[11]

The assets of a business entity are normally held for either use or resale. There is therefore an argument to be made in support of valuations which reflect these two alternative courses of action – i.e. to use values appropriate to the purpose for which assets are held (as distinct from the single value approach described in earlier chapters). In these circumstances, it can be further argued that the upper limit to the value of an asset to the entity is its replacement cost, for that is as much as the entity will lose should it be deprived of it. This is the foundation of the value to the business concept.

As well as replacement cost (RC), there are two further values to be considered with regard to an entity's assets – economic value (PV) and net realizable value (NRV). It is these three values which require to be constantly considered with regard to the purposes to which the assets should be put – i.e. whether they should be held for use or resale. In particular, the relationship of the values one to another will form the basis of such considerations. There are, in fact, six different combinations to be examined:

(1) PV > RC  > NRV          (4) NRV > PV  > RC
(2) PV > NRV > RC          (5) NRV > RC  > PV
(3) RC > PV  > NRV          (6) RC  > NRV > PV

Assets will be held for use in circumstances where their PV exceeds their NRV (the present value of their anticipated cash returns is greater than their estimated or known sale proceeds); and for resale when the reverse is the case. Thus, cases 1, 2 and 3 represent assets held for use within the entity, and cases 4, 5 and 6 represent those held by it for resale (case 6 in fact representing assets in which the entity is in the process of disinvestment). The proponents of the theory would further argue that, given the irrelevance of NRVs to the 'use' cases, and PV to the 'resale' cases (and remembering that RC is the upper valuation limit), the six situations can be restated as:

(1) RC          (4) RC
(2) RC          (5) RC
(3) RC > PV     (6) RC > NRV

This would mean that RC would form the basis of valuation in four of the six cases, with PV used in case 3 and NRV used in case 6. Thus, if this format is accepted, replacement costs would be the basis of asset valuation in most instances (except where an asset is worth using but not replacing, or is awaiting sale without replacement). This gives rise to the 'value to the business' valuation rule which is part of UK current cost accounting practice – the value of an asset is the lower of its replacement cost and the higher of its economic value and net realizable value. In addition, it results in measures of periodic income which are derived after allowing for the consumption of assets at their value to the business.

The validity of the above argument is debatable, and has been the subject of numerous comments and criticisms. The number of points made about the value to the business concept are so varied as to make it impossible to do them all justice within the limits of this chapter and text. However, a few of the main ones will be mentioned in order to provide the reader with an understanding that the use of the concept in practice is not as fully supported in the literature as the professional pronouncements might imply.

Following an earlier brief criticism of the concept within a different context, Chambers[12] produced the first major critique of it, arguing that the value to the business of an asset was its economic value (the maximum that it would pay for it) and that, by comparison, replacement cost and net realizable value were the values the market placed upon it. As such, he further argued, it was a valuation basis of relevance to entity management rather than to investors and other interested external parties. Gray and Wells[13] continued this theme, criticizing the advocates of value to the business for pre-empting hold, use and sell decisions on assets by the elimination of economic values and net realizable values from certain of the value relationships described above. As such, they appeared to support Chambers in his general view that the concept was more appropriate to management (and, thus, for asset decisions rather than income measurements). In fact, they regarded replacement costs as irrelevant (once the decision to hold, buy or sell the asset had been made) and that, given the subjectivity of economic value, only net realizable values should be considered for accounting purposes. This single valuation approach was attacked by Whittington[14] who argued for the need to use the concept of value to the business (and all three current values) for the purposes of asset decisions, thereby inferring its irrelevance for income measurement (as income measures are irrelevant for asset decisions).

Yoshida[15] lent his support to critics such as Chambers, Gray and Wells, and Whittington, particularly in his refusal to accept the relevance of value to the business for asset measurement purposes. According to him, the latter function concerns matters which have occurred, rather than future events and hypothetical losses (which are the basis of value to the business). Macdonald[16] took the debate a stage further. He distinguished between two interpretations of the concept – deprival value (in which the loss of assets is known – as in their consumption during business activity – and when value to the business can therefore be used in determining income), and value to the owner (in which the loss of assets is hypothesized, and value to the business becomes irrelevant for income and capital purposes). A further compromise was suggested by Popoff[17] – ignore economic value by assuming PV>RC; account for an asset on a replacement cost basis so long as there are current operating profits from it; and as soon as current operating losses arise, account for the asset on a net realizable value basis.

The lack of economic and business realism in the concept of value to the business was the subject of a critique by Wanless.[18] In particular, she objected to its assumptions of continuous entity equilibrium and profitability; and of its ability to respond instantly to value changes in order to maximize profitability. Gee and Peasnell,[19] on the other hand, have examined the value to the business notation, relationships and arguments described at the beginning of this section, and concluded that, in the case of RC>PV>NRV, the use of replacement cost as a surrogate for economic value is justified and, in the case of RC>NRV>PV, such a relationship is unlikely to happen. Thus, they further argue for the use of replacement cost in all cases, and that the concept of value to the business is consequently not required. Finally, Ma[20] has criticized the concept on the grounds of its variability (values changing as business optimism changes), and its ambiguity (the difficulty of attributing specific values to it).

Despite the above and other objections to it, the concept of value to the business has gained wide acceptance and, as previously mentioned, is utilized in practice. It is to the latter application that the next sections are devoted.

## Current cost accounting

In order to illustrate the application of the concept of value to the business, and the use of a mixture of current values, it is proposed to use a relevant past pronouncement of a professional accounting body.[21] This section outlines the main provisions of the pronouncement, at first using *ad hoc* illustrations of various parts of it, followed by a unified example based on the business situation and data utilized throughout the text. (Non-UK readers might like to adapt these examples to the corresponding pronouncements of their own countries.)

*Statement of Standard Accounting Practice 16* (1980) contained the following abbreviated provisions:

**1** An income statement, balance sheet, and supporting notes should be produced on a current cost accounting basis (using value to the business).

**2** In the income statement, cost of goods sold and depreciation of fixed assets should be accounted for on a value to the business basis, and the effects of price changes on monetary working capital (usually defined as debtors minus creditors) should also be provided for.

**3** Income, computed after making the adjustments in 2, should be augmented by a 'gearing' factor representing that proportion of the total adjustments financed by borrowings – i.e. leaving income as that attributable to the owners of the business.

**4** Value to the business should be defined as either net replacement cost or, if there has been a permanent diminution in value below the latter, the recoverable amount (the higher of net realizable value and the aggregate of anticipated net cash flows from use of the asset concerned). The latter 'valuation' is intended as a practical solution to the problem of discounting to obtain economic value.

**5** All unrealized value to the business changes, and all income statement provisions (in excess of the equivalent historic cost data, and net
of the gearing factor), should be transferred to a current cost reserve
(i.e. except reductions to recoverable amounts which should be
charged direct to the income statement).

The effects of these provisions are relatively clear – income is measured in terms of sales revenues minus the current cost of all assets
consumed (a form of current operating profit, henceforth termed
current cost operating profit); the balance sheet is updated into current
cost terms (because the valuation basis is value to the business,
replacement cost will be the usual form of measurement); all holding
gains (realized and unrealized) are not to be treated as income in the
first instance, being transferred to a separate reserve; and the maintenance of capital is in terms of the operating capability of the entity
financed by its owners (i.e. a combination of physical resource and
proprietary approaches to capital maintenance, thus making both it
and the valuation function of a mixed nature). The following illustrations are given in support of these points. The figures in each example
are not intended to be taken from the same business situation.

*1  Accounting for cost of sales and inventory*
  Assume inventory at $t_0$ was £1,000 (in historic cost terms). The
  equivalent figure at $t_1$ was £2,000, with goods being purchased
  during the period $t_0 - t_1$ for £5,000. It is estimated that the cost of
  sales (in value to the business terms) for the period $t_0 - t_1$ was £4,500,
  and the value to the business of inventory at $t_1$ was £2,600.

The historic cost of sales for the period $t_0 - t_1$ would be
£1,000+5,000−2,000 = £4,000; and the current cost of sales for the
same period would be £4,500. The difference between the two figures
of £500 would be the additional cost of sales to be deducted from sales
revenue in arriving at the current cost operating profit for the period,
and would also be added to the current cost reserve at $t_1$. In addition,
for balance sheet purposes, the inventory at $t_1$ would be revalued at
£2,600, and the £600 revaluation surplus would be transferred to the
current cost reserve.

*2  Accounting for depreciation and fixed assets*
  Assume plant was purchased at $t_0$ for £2,000 and was to be written
  off evenly over five periods (with an estimated nil scrap value).
  Assume also its value to the business at $t_1$ was a replacement cost of
  £2,500.

For balance sheet purposes at $t_1$, the plant would be included initially at its historic cost of £2,000 minus aggregate depreciation of 1/5 of £2,000 – i.e. at a net figure of £1,600. The traditional accounting income figure for the period $t_0-t_1$ would have been computed after providing for the depreciation of £400. To convert these figures into value to the business terms, the balance sheet figure of £1,600 for plant would be revalued to £2,000 (replacement cost £2,500 – aggregate depreciation £500), with the surplus of £400 being taken to the current cost reserve at $t_1$. Similarly, in the relevant income statement, an additional depreciation provision for the period $t_0-t_1$ of £100 (£500−400) would be made, with a corresponding addition to the current cost reserve being required at $t_1$.

### 3 Accounting for monetary working capital

Assume monetary working capital as the difference between debtors and creditors at each date. At $t_0$, monetary working capital was £6,000 and, at $t_1$, it had risen to £8,700. Assume also that the index movement for the period $t_0-t_1$ for such monetary items was from 100 to 120 with an average point of 110.

The total increase in monetary working capital for the period $t_0-t_1$ was £8,700−6,000 = £2,700. By adjusting the opening and closing figures to an average value to the business for the period (using the average movement in the relevant index), it is possible to segregate the price change from the 'volume' change. Thus, adjusting by the index, monetary working capital at $t_0$ becomes £6,000×110/100 = £6,600; and at $t_1$ becomes £8,700×110/120 = £8,000 (approximately). The 'volume' change for the period is therefore £8,000−6,600 = £1,400, and the price change, £1,300, giving the total movement of £2,700. The figure of £1,300 would be deducted from trading surpluses in arriving at the current cost operating profit, and added to the current cost reserve at $t_1$.

### 4 Accounting for the gearing adjustment

Assume at $t_1$ the following current cost data for the period $t_0-t_1$: additional current cost of sales, £700; additional current cost depreciation, £1,600; a price increase in monetary working capital, £200; average borrowings (other than creditors), £8,000; and average owner's capital and reserves (after revaluation of assets on a value to the business basis), £12,000.

The gearing factor at $t_1$ would be based on the relationship between borrowings and capital – i.e. £8,000/8,000+12,000 = 40%. Therefore, income, computed after deductions of £700+1,600+200 = £2,500, would be augmented by 40% of £2,500, thus defining it as that which is attributable to the owners of the business. The net adjustment to income for period $t_0-t_1$ of £2,500−1,500 = £1,000 would be transferred to the current cost reserve at $t_1$.

Each of the above adjustments has a specific objective – those relating to cost of sales and fixed asset depreciation have been met already within the context of replacement cost accounting (the additional current cost provisions representing the elimination from historic cost income of 'realized' holding gains on inventory and fixed assets in order to derive the operating gain of the period). The monetary working capital adjustment, on the other hand, has not appeared in any other income model. It is aimed at eliminating from historic cost income the inflationary effect on net monetary resources of the entity, thereby allowing the measurement of its current cost operating profits after provision has been made for the price changes affecting all of its operating resources. It is therefore regarded as an essential part of preserving the operating capability of the entity – this being defined in terms of fixed assets, inventory and monetary working capital. Such an adjustment, however, is not without its problems – there are obvious difficulties associated with the determination of the assets and liabilities which constitute monetary working capital (e.g., is a bank overdraft to be regarded as a current liability or a long-term borrowing?). Much will obviously depend on the circumstances of the individual entity.

Finally, the 'gearing' adjustment is intended to introduce a proprietorial influence on capital maintenance in current cost accounting. The limitation of current cost adjustments to those attributable to the owners of the entity thereby determines income in terms of the latter persons, and makes those holding gains said to be financed by borrowings available for possible distribution to the owners. It can also be argued that the 'gearing' adjustment makes some very uncertain assumptions about the present and future funding of assets (which assets are financed by which sources, and will these sources be available for funding in the future in the existing proportions?).

### Current cost income in practice

Using the business situation used throughout Chapters 4, 6 and 7, together with additional necessary data, it is now possible to provide an extended example of mixed value-based income determination. As in the previous section, the measurement principles are based on those contained in *Statement of Standard Accounting Practice 16* (1980). The situation details are as follows:

**Table 1**

| Time | Van | | | Shop | | |
|---|---|---|---|---|---|---|
| | Replacement cost* £ | Net realizable value £ | Future cash flows† £ | Replacement cost** £ | Net realizable value £ | Future cash flows† £ |
| $t_1$ | 1,050 | 850 | >1,050 | 6,000 | 5,700 | >6,000 |
| $t_2$ | 850 | 350 | >850 | 7,500 | 7,000 | >7,500 |
| $t_3$ | 450 | 100 | 100 | 10,000 | 9,500 | 9,500 |

* Net of relevant depreciation to date: $t_1$, £1,400 − 350; $t_2$, £1,700 − 850; $t_3$, £1,800 − 1,350.
** Stated at gross amount as no depreciation was provided.
† Approximate estimates made by management.

*Note:* At $t_3$, any reduction in asset value below net replacement cost should be regarded as permanent because of the near-future cessation of use of the asset concerned.

A business opened at $t_0$ with the purchase of a motor van for £1,200 and a shop for £5,000; cash operating surpluses before depreciation were £2,000 for the period $t_0-t_1$, £2,500 for the period $t_1-t_2$, and £1,700 for the period $t_2-t_3$. Business operations ceased immediately after $t_3$ when the van was sold for £100 and the shop for £10,300. Depreciation of the van was to be written off over four years on a straight-line basis with an estimated nil scrap value. In addition, the following data were available for purposes of computing relevant values to the business.

For purposes of computing value to the business at each date for each asset, the figures in Table 1 would require to be compared (following the valuation rule of the lower of net replacement cost and the recoverable amount – assuming relevant permanent diminutions in value). Replacement costs are net of any necessary depreciation provisions, and the future cash flows are aggregated but not discounted. Illustration 18 outlines the resultant computations. The accompanying commentary is divided into three main parts.

**Illustration 18  The computation of current cost income**

(a) *Current cost operating profits*

| | Period | | | | |
|---|---|---|---|---|---|
| | $t_0-t_1$ £ | $t_1-t_2$ £ | $t_2-t_3$ £ | $t_3-t_4$ £ | Total £ |
| Income before depreciation | 2,000 | 2,500 | 1,700 | — | 6,200 |
| *Less:* historic cost depreciation | 300[a] | 300[b] | 300[c] | 200[d] | 1,100 |
| | 1,700 | 2,200 | 1,400 | (200) | 5,100 |
| *Less:* current cost adjustments: additional current cost depreciation on van | 50 [e] | 125 [f] | 150 [g] | — | 325 |
| reduction from replace-cost to recoverable amount of van | — | — | 350 [h] | — | 350 |
| loss on realization of van not required | — | — | — | (200) [i] | (200) |
| | 50 | 125 | 500 | (200) | 475 |
| *Current cost operating profits* | 1,650 | 2,075 | 900 | — | 4,625 |

(a) $\frac{1}{4}\times$£1,200; (b) $\frac{1}{4}\times$£1,200; (c) $\frac{1}{4}\times$£1,200; (d) £1,200−900−100;
(e) $\frac{1}{4}\times$£1,400−£300; (f) $\frac{1}{4}\times$£1,700−£300; (g) $\frac{1}{4}\times$£1,800−£300;
(h) £1,800−1,350−100; (i) reversal of item (d).

*Illustration 18a:* A major purpose of current cost accounting is to measure periodic current cost operating profit – i.e. by starting with historic cost profits after depreciation, and then providing for relevant additional current costs. In this case, the latter relate solely to the depreciation of the van. First, in each of the three main periods, it is necessary to compute any additional current cost depreciation in excess of historic cost depreciation (in periods $t_0-t_1$, $t_1-t_2$ and $t_2-t_3$, this means calculating depreciation on a replacement cost basis, and then comparing this with the corresponding historic cost figure – e.g., in period $t_0-t_1$, current cost depreciation is $\frac{1}{4}\times£1,400 = £350$ and, with historic cost depreciation already deducted of £300, this results in an additional charge of £50. In both periods $t_0-t_1$ and $t_1-t_2$, the value to the business rule means the use of replacement costs for both depreciation and balance sheet purposes (the recoverable amount in each case being higher than the depreciated replacement cost). However, in period $t_2-t_3$, after providing for current cost depreciation, the valuation rule at $t_3$ compares a net replacement cost of £450 with a recoverable amount of £100 (the net realizable value). The difference of £350 requires to be written off against income for period $t_2-t_3$. Finally, as the van has been written down to its net realizable value of £100 at $t_3$, it is no longer necessary in period $t_3-t_4$ to provide for the historic cost loss on realization of £200. This has therefore been eliminated from the computation of current cost operating profit for that period.

*Illustration 18b:* The next matter to be considered is the composition of the transfers to the current cost reserve. In the case of the shop (which is not depreciated), these are relatively straightforward. During the period $t_0-t_1$ and $t_1-t_2$, the value to the business rule results in the use of replacement costs of £6,000 and £7,500, respectively (and in unrealized holding gains of £1,000 and £1,500, respectively). However, in period $t_2-t_3$, the value to the business of the shop is its net realizable value of £9,500 (an unrealized holding gain resulting of £2,000). In the final period $t_3-t_4$, the sale of the shop produces a realized gain of £800 (£10,300−9,500).

So far as the van is concerned, the first stage is to compute the unrealized changes in the value to the business (notes (e), (f) and (g)). In periods $t_0-t_1$, $t_1-t_2$ and $t_2-t_3$, this represents the change in gross replacement cost – from £1,200 (at $t_0$) to £1,400 (at $t_1$) to £1,700 (at $t_2$) to £1,800 (at $t_3$). In addition, adjustments require to be made to include the previously unrecorded aggregate depreciation provisions on these new asset values (notes (h), (i) and (j)) – e.g., at $t_1$, aggregate (*b*) *Current cost reserve*

|  | Time | | | |
|---|---|---|---|---|
|  | $t_1$ £ | $t_2$ £ | $t_3$ £ | $t_{3+}$ £ |
| Opening balance brought forward | — | 1,200 | 2,925 | 4,975 |
| *Add:* change in value of shop: |  |  |  |  |
| unrealized | 1,000[a] | 1,500[b] | 2,000[c] | — |
| realized | — | — | — | 800[d] |
| change in value of van: |  |  |  |  |
| unrealized | 200[e] | 300[f] | 100[g] | — |
| realized | (50)[h] | (200)[i] | (200)[j] | — |
| additional current cost depreciation on van | 50[k] | 125[l] | 150[m] | — |
|  | 1,200 | 2,925 | 4,975 | 5,775 |
| *Less:* distribution on cessation of business | — | — | — | 5,775 |
| *Closing balance carried forward* | 1,200 | 2,925 | 4,975 | — |

(a) £6,000−5,000; (b) £7,500−6,000; (c) £9,500−7,500; (d) £10,300−9,500;
(e) £1,400−1,200; (f) £1,700−1,400; (g) £1,800−1,700; (h) $\frac{1}{4} \times$£1,400−$\frac{1}{4} \times$£1,200;
(i) $\frac{1}{4} \times$£1,700−(£350+300); (j) $\frac{1}{2} \times$£1,800−(£850+300); (k) $\frac{1}{4} \times$£1,400−£300;
(l) $\frac{1}{4} \times$£1,700−£300; (m) $\frac{1}{2} \times$£1,800−£300.

depreciation is £300 ($\frac{1}{4} \times$£1,200) when it is required to be £350 ($\frac{1}{4} \times$£1,400); similarly, at $t_2$, it is £650 (£350 from $t_1$ plus the historic cost depreciation for period $t_1 - t_2$ of £300) and required to be £850 ($\frac{1}{2} \times$£1,700). Finally, as well as transferring the net changes in the value to the business of depreciable assets (as just described), it is necessary also to include the reductions in historic cost income which result from additional current cost depreciation (notes (k), (l) and (m) and already described in relation to Illustration 18a). It should be noted that these adjustments result in an overstatement of income for purposes of maintaining the capital of the entity in terms of operating capability. This is due entirely to the effective deduction of backlog depreciation from the reserve instead of operating profits. (The explanation, figures and alternative treatment are identical with those given on page 87 in relation to replacement cost accounting).

*Illustration 18c:* The purpose of this section of the Illustration is to

(c) *Total current cost income*

|  | Period | | | | |
|--|--|--|--|--|--|
|  | $t_0-t_1$ £ | $t_1-t_2$ £ | $t_2-t_3$ £ | $t_3-t_4$ £ | Total £ |
| Current operating profits[a] | 1,650 | 2,075 | 900 | — | 4,625 |
| Realized and unrealized holding gains taken to current cost reserve[b] | 1,200 | 1,725 | 2,050 | 800 | 5,775 |
| Current cost income | 2,850 | 3,800 | 2,950 | 800 | 10,400 |

(a) See 18a above; (b) See 18b above – $t_0-t_1$, £1,200−0; $t_1-t_2$, £2,925−1,200; $t_2-t_3$, £4,975−2,925; $t_3-t_4$, £5,775−4,975.

demonstrate that, if operating and holding gains are aggregated, the resultant total (in this case termed current cost income) can be computed in a similar way to the business and realizable totals described earlier. A comparison can then be made with these other income models. It reveals that, for periods $t_0-t_1$ and $t_1-t_2$, total income (£2,850 and £3,800) is identical to that in the business income model (because, in both models and for both periods, the valuation basis used is replacement cost); for period $t_2-t_3$, the income figure of £2,950 is dissimilar to both its business income (£3,800) and its realizable income (£3,950) counterparts (because it has used a mixture of replacement costs and realizable values); and for period $t_3-t_4$, the income figure is identical to the realizable income figure (£800) (because, by $t_3$, the current cost model in this case utilizes the realizable value basis).

*Illustration 18d:* This final section on current cost accounting describes the relevant value to the business adjustments to the balance sheet. Most of these movements have already been described in sections 18a and 18b in relation to the changes in value of the van and the shop – i.e. in each case at $t_1$ and $t_2$, to replacement costs; and at $t_3$, to recoverable amounts. The figures for retained income and the current cost reserve are cumulative and derived from sections 18a and 18b, respectively. The illustration also demonstrates that, as with other income models, periodic income can be equated with the periodic change in measured capital.

(*d*) *Financial position on a current cost basis*

| | Time | | | | |
|---|---|---|---|---|---|
| | $t_0$<br>£ | $t_1$<br>£ | $t_2$<br>£ | $t_3$<br>£ | $t_4$<br>£ |
| Shop | 5,000 | 6,000[a] | 7,500[b] | 9,500[c] | — |
| Van | 1,200 | 1,050[d] | 850[e] | 100[f] | — |
| Cash | — | 2,000[g] | 4,500[h] | 6,200[i] | —[j] |
| | 6,200 | 9,050 | 12,850 | 15,800 | — |
| Original capital | 6,200 | 6,200 | 6,200 | 6,200 | — |
| Current cost reserve | — | 1,200[k] | 2,925[k] | 4,975[k] | — |
| Retained income | — | 1,650[l] | 3,725[m] | 4,625[n] | — |
| *Capital* | 6,200 | 9,050 | 12,850 | 15,800 | —[o] |
| *Increase in capital* | — | 2,850[p] | 3,800[q] | 2,950[r] | (15,800)[s] |

(a) £5,000+1,000; (b) £6,000+1,500; (c) £7,500+2,000; (d) £1,400−$\frac{1}{4}$×£1,400;
(e) £1,700−$\frac{1}{2}$×£1,700; (f) £1,800−$\frac{3}{4}$×£1,800−£350; (g) £0+2,000;
(h) £2,000+2,500; (i) £4,500+1,700; (j) £6,200+10,300+100−16,600; (k) as in 18b
above; (l) £0+1,650; (m) £1,650+2,075; (n) £3,725+900;
(o) £6,200+4,975+800−16,600; (p) £9,050−6,200; (q) £12,850−9,050;
(r) £15,800−12,850; (s) £0−15,800.

## The advantages and disadvantages of mixed values

Many of the advantages (for example, the use of contemporary values)
and the disadvantages (for example, the difficulty of knowing how to
treat holding gains) of the 'single value' current value models are just
as relevant to the mixed value model, and it is therefore not intended to
repeat them in this chapter. However, the use of mixed values brings
with it attendant problems which ought to be seriously considered
when judging its merits. It should be noted that these problems are
cited within the general context of current cost accounting, and the use
therein of mixed values in the application of the value to the business
rule. They are not given as specific comments on particular systems of
such accounting.

**1** Value to the business is a relatively ambiguous valuation rule – at
least in terms of its definition. It appears to be concerned with the use

of value data in order to make decisions about the buying, holding and selling of assets. Yet it is recommended as a means of measuring the results of past activity. As such, there is a contradiction in its use for income and measurement purposes. In part, it is truthful in its description of the assets of the business entity – some will be held for use (and then replaced); some will be held for resale (and then replaced); and some will be sold (without replacement). However, these are all hypothetical events – they have not occurred and, meantime, at the time of accounting, they are being held by the entity. There is therefore a strong case in these circumstances for suggesting that the value to the business of its assets, at the time of accounting, is their economic value.

2 A further interpretation of the concept of value to the business concerns its notion of the entity being deprived of its assets. Again, this is entirely hypothetical as, at the time of accounting, deprival has not taken place. It is therefore questionable whether such a notion is relevant to income and capital measurements for those persons interested in receiving information about the progress and financial position of the entity. It may, however, have some relevance to internal management concerned when answering the question, 'What if we were deprived of these assets?'

The importance of the notion of deprival in this concept stems from its original legal origin concerning judicial reparation for lost property. The doubt is therefore whether a legal idea can be easily and relevantly transplanted into accounting.

3 The mixed value approach to income determination results in a heterogeneous mixture of asset values being used to compute current value income. The meaningfulness of the aggregate valuation of the resultant capital figure therefore appears to be in doubt. It contains current values, but not the same type of current values, and it may therefore be argued (on the grounds of the need to ensure proper additivity of data) that the aggregation of different types of current value produces capital and income figures which are relatively meaningless (except in situation where there is little difference between entry and exit prices). In reply, it can be argued that all that is being aggregated is values to the business and, thus, there is additivity. However, this does not provide a satisfactory answer to the meaning of the total capital figure, and it ignores the problems of defining value to the business mentioned in 1 and 2 above.

4 The realism of the value to the business concept must also be questioned in terms of the assumptions and influences it makes – for

example, that entities are profitable, are in a state of relative equilibrium in a disequilibrium world, and can adapt instantaneously to events affecting their asset values. The users of the concept must judge the reasonableness of these matters.

5 Finally, in the sense that the use of the value to the business concept will result, in most instances, in the application of replacement cost accounting, it obviously has the advantages of the latter model. It does attempt to segregate operating from holding gains; it does produce a 'current value' balance sheet; it is feasible to implement in practice (witness recent published financial reports of quoted UK companies); and it is attempting to describe the activities of the entity for its various user groups. It is also based on traditional accounting income and, as such, can be easily related to the latter. However, there are arguments against it which are serious enough to impinge on any judgement of its overall utility.

## References

(See page 179 for Selected Bibliography)

1. K. MacNeal, *Truth in Accounting,* Scholars Book Co., 1970 (reprint), p. 172.

2. R. T. Sprouse and M. Moonitz, *Accounting Research Study 3,* American Institute of Certified Public Accountants, 1962, pp. 23–36.

3. H. Ross, *Financial Statements–A Crusade for Current Values,* Pitman, 1969, pp. 29–41.

4. Arthur Andersen & Co., *Objectives of Financial Statements for Business Enterprises,* Arthur Andersen & Co., 1972, pp. 52–6.

5. J. R. Grinyer and R. W. Lewis, 'Valuation and Meaningful Accounts', *Accounting and Business Research,* Autumn 1972, pp. 275–83.

6. J. C. Bonbright, *The Valuation of Property,* McGraw Hill, 1937.

7. F. K. Wright, 'Towards a General Theory of Depreciation', *Journal of Accounting Research,* Spring 1964, pp. 80–90.

8. D. Solomons, 'Economic and Accounting Concepts of Cost and Value', in M. Backer (ed.), *Modern Accounting Theory,* Prentice Hall, 1966, pp. 117–40.

9. E. Stamp, 'Income and Value Determination and Changing Price-Levels: an Essay Towards a Theory', *Accountant's Magazine,* June 1971, pp. 277–92.

10. W. T. Baxter, *Accounting Values and Inflation,* McGraw Hill, 1975, pp. 116–44.

11. The arguments put forward in this section represent the main ones utilized by the advocates of mixed values. The author, as elsewhere in the text, does not necessarily agree with them.

12. R. J. Chambers, 'Value to the Owner', *Abacus,* June 1971, pp. 62–72.

13. S. J. Gray and M. C. Wells, 'Asset Values and Ex Post Income', *Accounting and Business Research,* Summer 1973, pp. 163–7.

14. G. Whittington, 'Asset Valuation, Income Measurement and Accounting Income', *Accounting and Business Research,* Spring 1974, pp. 96–101.

15. H. Yoshida, 'Value to the Firm and the Asset Measurement Problem', *Abacus,* June 1973, pp. 16–21.

16. G. Macdonald, 'Deprival Value: Its Use and Abuse', *Accounting and Business Research,* Autumn 1974, pp. 263–9.

17. B. Popoff, 'The Informational Value of Replacement Cost Accounting in External Company Reports', *Accounting and Business Research,* Winter 1974, pp. 61–70.

18. P. T. Wanless, 'Reflections on Asset Valuations and Value to the Firm', *Abacus,* December 1974, pp. 160–64.

19. K. P. Gee and K. V. Peasnell, 'A Pragmatic Defence of Replacement Cost', *Accounting and Business Research,* Autumn 1976, pp. 242–9.

20. R. Ma, 'Value to the Owner Revisited', *Abacus,* December 1976, pp. 159–65.

21. Accounting Standards Committee, *Statement of Standard Accounting Practice 16* 1980.

# 9 Current value income and economic income

The text has so far concentrated primarily on analysing the three main current value income models, and their individual relationships, in contrast to the traditional accounting model. To complete this comparative analysis, it seems appropriate to examine the relationship of the current value incomes with economic income in much the same way as was done when comparing the latter concept with traditional accounting income in Chapter 4.

The basic relationship between current value income and economic income results from the corresponding relationship between current and economic values. The difference between the current value and economic value of an investment or an entity was originally described by Edwards and Bell[1] as subjective goodwill – i.e. the excess of economic value over current value which arises because the investor values the investment or the entity concerned more highly than the market values the underlying resources. This is the *raison d'être* for investing; if subjective goodwill did not exist, then there is no reason for the investor to invest. Thus, for example (in an entity situation), at point t, $PV_t - CV_t = SGW_t$; where $PV_t$ is the economic value of the entity (measured in subjective discounted future benefit terms); $CV_t$ is the current value of the entity (measured in market-based value terms); and $SGW_t$ is the subjective goodwill which the investor places upon the entity, over and above the aggregate of the various resource market values. (Subjective goodwill is, therefore, simply another form of 'windfall' gain of the type already met and discussed in Chapters 3 and 4; particularly with regard to its treatment and classification as income or capital.)

As Edwards and Bell[2] point out, however, the subjective goodwill which the investor sees at the time of investing gradually diminishes in value as it is converted into market values, owing to the eventual realization of the previously anticipated benefits. It is this change in the value of subjective goodwill over the lifetime of the investment or entity concerned which is central to the relationship between current value and economic incomes. Assuming the subjective goodwill identity above, the following notation identifies this relationship and the gradual expiry of goodwill value over a definite life-time. Assume, also, for the sake of simplicity, that the business entity makes no distributions until the end of that life-time.

First, $Y_e = K_t - K_{t-1}$; where $Y_e$ is the economic income of the entity for the period $t-1$ to $t$; $K_t$ is the capital of the entity at the end of the period, measured in present value terms; and $K_{t-1}$ is the capital of the entity at the beginning of the period, also measured in present value terms.

Secondly, $Y_c = R_t - R_{t-1}$; where $Y_c$ is the current value income of the entity for the period $t-1$ to $t$; $R_t$ is the capital of the entity at the end of the period, measured in current value terms; $R_{t-1}$ is the capital of the entity at the beginning of the period, also measured in current value terms; and, once again, assuming no new capital or loan receipts or repayments.

Thirdly, $K_t - R_t = SGW_t$; where $K_t$ is the capital of the entity at point $t$, measured in present value terms; $R_t$ is the capital of the entity at point $t$, measured in current value terms; and $SGW_t$ is the subjective goodwill at point $t$.

From the above assumptions it can therefore be seen that:

$$Y_e - Y_c = (K_t - K_{t-1}) - (R_t - R_{t-1}) = (K_t - R_t) - (K_{t-1} - R_{t-1})$$
$$= SGW_t - SGW_{t-1} = \Delta SGW_{((t-1)-t)};$$

where $\Delta SGW$ is the periodic change in the value of the subjective goodwill of the entity.
Therefore,

$$Y_e - \Delta SGW = Y_c$$

Thus the relationship between economic and current value income is the periodic change in subjective goodwill arising from its translation from subjective discounted anticipations to realized market values. Over the life of the entity or investment concerned, therefore, the value of $\Delta SGW$ in the above identity would tend to be negative – representative, that is, of a fall in the value of subjective goodwill, as Illustrations 19, 20 and 21 confirm, using the situation and figures already used throughout the chapters dealing with accounting, busi-

**Table 2**

| Period | Business income £ | Realizable income £ | Current cost income £ | Time | Replacement cost capital £ | Realizable value capital £ | Current cost capital £ |
|---|---|---|---|---|---|---|---|
| $t_0-t_1$ | 2,850 | 2,350 | 2,850 | $t_0$ | 6,200 | 6,200 | 6,200 |
| $t_1-t_2$ | 3,800 | 3,300 | 3,800 | $t_1$ | 9,050 | 8,550 | 9,050 |
| $t_2-t_3$ | 3,800 | 3,950 | 2,950 | $t_2$ | 12,850 | 11,850 | 12,850 |
| $t_3-t_4$ | (50) | 800 | 800 | $t_3$ | 16,650 | 15,800 | 15,800 |
|  |  |  |  | $t_4$ | — | — | — |
|  | 10,400 | 10,400 | 10,400 |  |  |  |  |

ness, realizable, and current cost incomes. Illustration 19 examines the relationship between economic and business incomes (the_above notation does not specify which current value is applicable; in fact, replacement costs, net realizable values, and values to the business are equally applicable). Illustration 20 (page 127) will conduct a similar examination of economic and realizable incomes, and Illustration 21 (page 128) will deal with economic and current cost incomes.

The background material is as given in Table 2. (Readers should refer to pages 78–85, for the computation of the business income model figures, to pages 94–7 for the realizable income model figures, and to pages 112–18 for the current cost income model figures.)

**Table 3**

| Period | Economic income £ | Time | Economic capital £ |
|--------|-------------------|------|--------------------|
| $t_0-t_1$ | 949 | $t_0$ | 13,550 |
| $t_1-t_2$ | 1,015 | $t_1$ | 14,499 |
| $t_2-t_3$ | 1,086 | $t_2$ | 15,514 |
| $t_3-t_4$ | — | $t_3$ | 16,600 |
| | 3,050 | $t_4$ | — |

In addition to this, it is also necessary to compute economic income and capital value for the same periods and times, and based upon the same situation and figures used for the above computations. This has already been done, in an ideal *ex post* sense, when comparing economic income with traditional accounting income (Chapter 4, pages 59–64), and the figures are therefore as given in Table 3.

The following comments explain the figures given in the illustration:

**1** At $t_0$, replacement cost capital is measured in terms of tangible resources only, and therefore is exceeded, to the extent of £7,350, by economic capital which includes intangible goodwill. The occurrence of this additional resource value results from the fact that the economic model is based on all anticipated future benefits, whereas the business income model is based solely on measured historic transactions. This situation is therefore identical to that already dealt with in Chapter 4 when comparing the accounting and economic models.

**Illustration 19  Business income and economic income**

| Time | Economic capital (K) £ | Replacement cost capital (R) £ | Change in subjective goodwill (ΔSGW) £ | Economic income ($Y_e$) £ | Business income ($Y_b$) £ |
|---|---|---|---|---|---|
| $t_0$ | 13,550 | 6,200 | 7,350 [a] | — | — |
| $t_1$ | 14,499 | 9,050 | (1,901) [b] | 949 | 2,850 |
| $t_2$ | 15,514 | 12,850 | (2,785) [c] | 1,015 | 3,800 |
| $t_3$ | 16,600 | 16,650 | (2,714) [d] | 1,086 | 3,800 |
| $t_4$ | — | — | 50 [e] | — | (50) |
|  |  |  |  | 3,050 | 10,400 |

(a) (£13,550−6,200)−(£0−0); (b) (£14,499−9,050)−(£13,550−6,200);
(c) (£15,514−12,850)−(£14,499−9,050);
(d) (£16,600−16,650)−(£15,514−12,850); (e) (£0−0)−(£16,600−16,650).

2 By comparing opening and closing economic and replacement cost capitals at the end of each period, the change in the original goodwill is measured (as in notes (a) to (e) inclusive). Following the identity $Y_e - \Delta SGW = Y_b$, the periodic change in goodwill (which is normally negative in value) can be deducted from economic income in order to equate with business income. In other words, business income is composed of two parts: economic income and realization of a portion of the original subjective goodwill; as was the case with accounting income (see pages 59–64). Thus, using the above data, the following reconciliation can be made.

| Period | $Y_e$ £ | − | $\Delta SGW$ £ | = | $Y_b$ £ |
|---|---|---|---|---|---|
| $t_0-t_1$ | 949 |  | (1,901) |  | 2,850 |
| $t_1-t_2$ | 1,015 |  | (2,785) |  | 3,800 |
| $t_2-t_3$ | 1,086 |  | (2,714) |  | 3,800 |
| $t_3-t_4$ | — |  | 50 |  | (50) |
|  | 3,050 |  | (7,350) |  | 10,400 |

3 It therefore follows that, in total, business income (£10,400) comprises realized economic income (£3,050) and realized goodwill (£7,350). Thus, business income does in fact include a possible return of economic capital which is not normally recognized in accounting practice because of its intangible nature; much, however, depends on how the 'windfall' of £7,350 is treated. As explained in Chapters 3 and 4, this can be regarded as income, capital, or a mixture of both. For reasons already given in Chapter 4, page 63, the figure for subjective goodwill is being treated as capital in this particular situation.

A similar exercise can be conducted with realizable income (Illustration 20). As was the case with business income, the original goodwill figure of £7,350, and its subsequent realized elements, are computed

**Illustration 20  Realizable income and economic income**

| Time | Economic capital (K) £ | Realizable capital (R) £ | Change in subjective goodwill ($\Delta$SGW) £ | Economic income ($Y_e$) £ | Realizable income ($Y_r$) £ |
|---|---|---|---|---|---|
| $t_0$ | 13,550 | 6,200 | 7,350 [a] | — | — |
| $t_1$ | 14,499 | 8,550 | (1,401)[b] | 949 | 2,350 |
| $t_2$ | 15,514 | 11,850 | (2,285)[c] | 1,015 | 3,300 |
| $t_3$ | 16,600 | 15,800 | (2,864)[d] | 1,086 | 3,950 |
| $t_4$ | — | — | (800)[e] | — | 800 |
| | | | | | |
| | | | | — | 3,050 | 10,400 |

(a) (£13,550−6,200)−(£0−0); (b) (£14,499−8,550)−(£13,550−6,200);
(c) (£15,514−11,850)−(£14,499−8,550);
(d) (£16,600−15,800)−(£15,514−11,850); (e) (£0−0)−(£16,600−15,800).

| Period | $Y_e$ £ | − | $\Delta$SGW £ | = | $Y_r$ £ |
|---|---|---|---|---|---|
| $t_0-t_1$ | 949 | | (1,401) | | 2,350 |
| $t_1-t_2$ | 1,015 | | (2,285) | | 3,300 |
| $t_2-t_3$ | 1,086 | | (2,864) | | 3,950 |
| $t_3-t_4$ | — | | (800) | | 800 |
| | 3,050 | | (7,350) | | 10,400 |

by making periodic comparisons of economic and current value capitals. Similarly, realizable income comprises two elements: economic income and the realization of a portion of the original subjective goodwill. This can be seen in the application of the basic identity $Y_e - \Delta SGW = Y_r$ to the above data.

Finally, the reconciliation of current cost and economic incomes can be conducted in similar fashion, with the changes in subjective goodwill proving to be the link between economic estimates and market-based prices. This is given in Illustration 21.

**Illustration 21   Current cost income and economic income**

| Time | Economic capital (K) £ | Current cost capital (R) £ | Change in subjective goodwill ($\Delta SGW$) £ | Economic income ($Y_e$) £ | Current cost income ($Y_{cc}$) £ |
|---|---|---|---|---|---|
| $t_0$ | 13,550 | 6,200 | 7,350 [a] | — | — |
| $t_1$ | 14,499 | 9,050 | (1,901) [b] | 949 | 2,850 |
| $t_2$ | 15,514 | 12,850 | (2,785) [c] | 1,015 | 3,800 |
| $t_3$ | 16,600 | 15,800 | (1,864) [d] | 1,086 | 2,950 |
| $t_4$ | — | — | (800) [e] | — | 800 |
| | | | | 3,050 | 10,400 |

(a) (£13,550−6,200)−(£0−0); (b) (£14,499−9,050)−(£13,550−6,200);
(c) (£15,514−12,850)−(£14,499−9,050);
(d) (£16,600−15,800)−(£15,514−12,850); (e) (£0−0)−(£16,600−15,800).

Reconciliation of the income data (using the identity $Y_e - \Delta SGW = Y_{cc}$) can be achieved as follows:

| Period | $Y_e$ £ | − | $\Delta SGW$ £ | = | $Y_{cc}$ £ |
|---|---|---|---|---|---|
| $t_0-t_1$ | 949 | | (1,901) | | 2,850 |
| $t_1-t_2$ | 1,015 | | (2,785) | | 3,800 |
| $t_2-t_3$ | 1,086 | | (1,864) | | 2,950 |
| $t_3-t_4$ | — | | (800) | | 800 |
| | 3,050 | | (7,350) | | 10,400 |

In summary, it may be said that the economic and current value income models are materially different: they use differing capital values and produce differing income figures, both periodically and in aggregate (but depending on the treatment of the 'windfall'). The current value models normally ignore the existence of intangible resources simply because they rarely appear as recordable historic transactions. This means that, over the lifetime of the entity concerned, each type of current value incomes may well contain elements of returns of economic capital representing such expired intangibles as managerial skills and experience. For this reason alone, it is hard to see the justification for using any of the current value models as a surrogate for the economic model. All models are complementary rather than competing, and it should be remembered that, despite its use in Illustrations 19, 20 and 21 as an entity concept, the economic model is primarily intended as a tool for analysing personal economic behaviour and for making rational economic decisions. On the other hand, each of the current value models is specifically intended to describe entity activity, and therefore is based on entity transactions. Thus, while these models may be advocated for decision functions, they still remain essentially stewardship or accountability orientated, producing income measures of past economic activity.

## References

(See pages 189–90 for Selected Bibliography)
1. E. O. Edwards and P. W. Bell, *The Theory and Measurement of Business Income*, University of California Press, 1961, pp. 33–69.
2. ibid., pp. 48–9.

# 10 The price-level problem

## The nature of the price-level problem

Previous chapters have described how income determination involves, first, valuing capital (either in economic or accounting terms); and, secondly, comparing the opening and closing capital values of a defined period to ensure that closing capital is maintained at the level of opening capital before income is recognized. In doing so, however, each chapter has assumed that opening and closing capitals have each been measured in the same monetary terms – i.e. that no part of the value increments concerned has been due to changes in the value of the monetary measurement unit. This chapter relaxes this assumption, and questions its validity.

Money, the so-called language of business, is the measurement unit commonly used in income and value determination. But as well as being a useful measurement unit, it is also a means of exchange for goods and services. The values of these goods and services are therefore expressed in terms of money, i.e. as market prices. For example, if a good has a market price of £2 at $t_0$, and a similar price of £3 at $t_1$, the assumption so far in this text has been that the value of the good has risen by 50 per cent, during the period $t_0 - t_1$. Such a price change is defined as a specific price change; i.e. specific to that particular good. However, this is to look only at the specific purchasing power of the £ in relation to that good. It is not indicative of the generalized purchasing power of the £ in terms of its value to goods and services in general.

General price movements or changes are, by definition, not specific to any particular good or service – except by accident. They may be said to be relevant to every good and service, and therefore to every consumer, because of their universality. Thus we come to the well-known problem of inflation (or deflation): the movement, usually downwards, of the generalized or average purchasing power of the monetary unit; the increase in money prices of goods and services which does not reflect a real increase in their value to the consumer. For instance, in the above simple example, if prices had risen in general during the period $t_0 - t_1$ by 10 per cent, then the value of the good at $t_0$, revised in terms of money values at $t_1$, would be £2·20; in other words, the general price increase would be £0·20. But the specific price change for the good was 50 per cent or £1. Therefore, this latter price movement may be divided into two parts: the general increase of £0·20 (not representative of any actual change in value because of its inflationary nature); and the relative increase of £0·80 (representative of a real increase in the value of the good).

From the above, it may be seen that there are three types of price changes: (a) general – the average of all price changes over a period, and representing the overall change in the value and purchasing power of money; (b) specific – the particular price change representing the change in the money value of a specific good or service (including, in part, any general price change which has occurred during the defined period because of an aggregation of specific price changes); and (c) relative – that part of a specific price change which remains after excluding from it any general price change that may also have occurred. All three types of change can be incorporated into the process of income determination. The purpose of this chapter is to explain how this is done; and, in particular, how general and relative price changes can be computed in the alternative economic, accounting and current value income models.

## General, specific and relative price restatement

The material already covered in previous chapters has shown evidence that income determination involves the recognition of prices and price changes. In each model, it is specific price changes which are accounted for when measuring the various realized and unrealized gains – specific, that is, to particular goods and services, and to particular business entities. However, because of the assumption of monetary stability made throughout these chapters, general price changes have not so far been taken into account. Thus, having accounted for specific changes, it is now important also to account for general changes and thereby attempt to recognize the effect on income and value measurements of changing money values. General price restatement procedures will now be applied to each of the various income models: economic income, accounting income, business income, realizable income, and current cost income.

It must always be kept in mind that general price restatement is not, of itself, an attempt to value capital in contemporary terms. (Such is the process of specific price restatement already described in each of the foregoing chapters on the various income models.) General price restatement is a monetary adjustment to allow for the effect of the fluctuating value of money. It is a form of 'optional extra' which can be incorporated into any of the economic or accounting income models. Its purpose is to eliminate from the periodic capital value increment that part which is an inflationary increase, which is (usually) due to the general movement in prices during the defined period, thereby leaving as income the residue of the value increment which arises from relative price movements reflecting real increases in capital. This process is achieved by restating the economic or accounting capital at the beginning of the period in the same general purchasing power terms as closing capital. This is done by multiplying opening capital by a factor representing the percentage increase in prices during the period concerned. It therefore becomes apparent that the process of general price restatement is part of the concept of capital maintenance so fundamental to income determination – i.e. capital is maintained in the same monetary purchasing power terms. It is not, however, part of the process of valuation which determines the capital values to which the concept of capital maintenance is then applied.

The problem of incorporating general price changes into the process of capital maintenance arises because of the ever-present problem of inflation. It has been ignored in the past largely because the problem of inflation has been only gradual. It is, however, a problem which is compounding and has come to demand urgent attention because of its cumulative effect over a number of years. The following may be summarized as the main reasons given in the standard literature to account for changes in the value of money:

1 General price restatement is said to provide more meaningful information because it enables periodic comparisons of income and value data to be made more realistically when expressed in the same monetary terms. This requires, however, that all comparable data be continuously updated into current purchasing power terms.

2 Following on from (1), it has also been said that not to segregate real from inflationary value increments in the process of income determination is to provide misleading and irrelevant information, inflation being a relevant and significant factor to the decision maker using the information.

**3** General price restatement is a more appropriate attempt at segregating inflationary effects than such traditional and haphazard methods (which, in fact, are valuation adjustments) as replacement cost depreciation.

**4** One of the basic assumptions of the traditional accounting income model is the monetary stability of the measurement unit. The obvious invalidity of this postulate has given rise to the advocacy of general price restatement.

**5** One of the primary measurement criteria in income determination (described in Chapter 2) is that there should be additivity of resource values in computing opening and closing capital. It is therefore argued that, unless these values are expressed in the same general purchasing power terms, there can be no additivity.

**6** Lastly, it is often argued that general price restatement is necessary to adjust for the effects of inflation so as to determine the real taxable capacity of the entity (it being unfair to tax 'fictitious' inflationary gains); the appropriate level of distributions and retentions of income (in order not to impair future operating capacity by overdistributing); and, more generally, investment and pricing policies of entity management (so as to compute an appropriate real return on capital employed).

## Restatement of economic income

The economic income model can be adjusted for the monetary effect of inflation, and this has been advocated by, among others, Hicks[1] and Fisher.[2] In conceptual terms, this may be shown as follows:

Take the basic economic model as $Y_e = C + (K_t - K_{t-1})$; where $Y_e$ is the economic income for the period $t-1$ to $t$; C is the realized cash flow of the same period, assumed to be realized at t; $K_t$ is the closing capital measured in terms of discounted future cash flows; and $K_{t-1}$ is a similar computation of capital at the beginning of the period. Also assume that prices have risen in general by a factor p during the period $t-1$ to t. Therefore, incorporating the general price adjustment into the basic identity, $Y_{\cdot e\cdot} = C + (K_t - K(1+p)_{t-1})$; where $Y_{\cdot e\cdot}$ is 'real' economic income and $K(1+p)_{t-1}$ is the opening capital expressed in the same general purchasing power terms as the closing capital $K_t$. C will also require to be inflated by a suitable factor of p if the initial assumption of receipt at point t is relaxed.

Table 4

| Period | C £ | $K_t$ £ | $K_{t-1}$ £ | $Y_e$ £ |
|--------|-----|---------|-------------|---------|
| $t_0-t_1$ | — | 14,499 | 13,550 | 949 |
| $t_1-t_2$ | — | 15,514 | 14,499 | 1,015 |
| $t_2-t_3$ | — | 16,600 | 15,514 | 1,086 |
| $t_3-t_4$ | 16,600 | — | 16,600 | — |
| | 16,600 | | | 3,050 |

**Illustration 22　Price-level restated economic income**

| Period | $C(1+p)$ $£_g$ | $K_t$ $£_g$ | $K(1+p)_{t-1}$ $£_g$ | $Y_{e'}$ $£_g$ |
|--------|----------------|-------------|----------------------|----------------|
| $t_0-t_1$ | — | 14,499 | 14,905[a] | (406) |
| $t_1-t_2$ | — | 15,514 | 15,949[b] | (435) |
| $t_2-t_3$ | — | 16,600 | 17,053[c] | (453) |
| $t_3-t_4$ | 18,223[d] | — | 18,223[e] | — |
| | 18,223 | | | (1,294) |

(a) £13,550×110/100; (b) $£_g$14,499×121/110;
(c) $£_g$15,514×133/121; (d) $£_g$16,600×146/133;
(e) $£_g$16,600×146/133.

| Period | $Y_{e'}(1+p)$ $£_g$ | = | $Y_{e'g}$ $£_g$ |
|--------|---------------------|---|-----------------|
| $t_0-t_1$ | (406)(1·3273)[a] | | (539) |
| $t_1-t_2$ | (435)(1·2066)[b] | | (525) |
| $t_2-t_3$ | (453)(1·0977)[c] | | (497) |
| | | | (1,561) |

(a) 146/110; (b) 146/121; (c) 146/133.

*Source:* This illustration, together with subsequent ones in this chapter, follows the restatement method in the now withdrawn *Provisional Statement of Standard Accounting Practice 7*, 1974 (unless otherwise stated in the relevant part of the text). The notation $£_g$ indicates a unit of purchasing power, and should be distinguished from £ which represents a unit of money.

This can be shown in more practical terms by taking the economic income and capital used in the comparative analysis in the previous chapter. The facts were as in Table 4 (using the notation defined above). It should also be assumed that the general price index at $t_0$ was 100, at $t_1$ 110, at $t_2$ 121, at $t_3$ 133, and at $t_4$ 146.

Illustration 22 reveals that a moderate period rate of inflation can cause significant changes to economic income measures when cognisance is taken of the latter factor. In this case, unadjusted income for the period, $t_0 - t_4$, was £3,050, but the equivalent restated figure for the same period was $£_g(1,561)$ (expressed in terms of $£_g$ at $t_4$). The periodic figures are determined by maintaining capital in terms of the same purchasing power – the constant 7 per cent money return on capital being reduced by a constant 10 per cent inflation rate to a constant negative 3 per cent real return on capital in each period. The validity of this example is, however, open to some doubt: first, because of the various assumptions which underlie the computation of economic income (already discussed in Chapter 3); secondly, because there is the question of adapting what is a personal income model to an entity situation (also examined in Chapter 3); and thirdly, because of the various assumptions made to simplify the illustration (e.g. the constancy of the rate of inflation). This notwithstanding, the example does show the misleading portrayal of income which can arise if the factor of inflation (or deflation) is not recognized and measured.

The income aggregate of $£_g(1,294)$ is misleading in the sense that it is expressed in terms of $£_g$ of different purchasing powers (thereby violating the additivity criterion). In order to correct this fault, each income datum should be re-expressed in terms of the purchasing power relevant at $t_4$. Thus, $Y_{·e'}$ multiplied by the relevant index change determines the readjusted income $Y_{·e'g}$ – i.e. $£_g(1,561)$.

## Restatement of accounting income

Since the restatement of traditional accounting income allows for changes in the value of money, it is a somewhat more complex process than that concerned with economic income, though the same general principle of restating opening capital applies. The technique is based on the fundamental distinction between monetary and non-monetary resources instead of the usual fixed and current asset classifications of traditional accounting. This is necessary if non-monetary resources are to be treated differently from monetary ones: the former are not in current monetary purchasing power terms (and therefore need to be restated), whereas the latter do not require restatement as they are already expressed in such terms. The following notation is a conceptual explanation of the process:

> First, assume $M_t + N_t = R_t + L_t$; where M are the monetary resources of the entity (i.e. mainly cash and debtors); N are its non-monetary resources (e.g. plant and machinery, and inventories of stocks and work in progress); R is its residual equity (including subscribed capital and retained income of previous periods); and L are its long-term and short-term liabilities. Secondly, assume also that during the period t to t+1, there were no operational or capital receipt and repayment transactions, and that the percentage general movement in prices during the same period was equivalent to a factor p. Therefore, applying, at t+1, the general price change p to the entity position expressed at t,

> $$M_t(1+p) + N_t(1+p) = R_t(1+p) + L_t(1+p)$$

> Therefore,

> $$M_t + M_t p + N_t(1+p) = R_t(1+p) + L_t + L_t p$$

> Restating still further, the final identity may be shown as:

> $$M_t + N_t(1+p) - L_t = R_t(1+p) - M_t p + L_t p$$

The above is therefore the restated accounting balance sheet identity – the original being expressed in money units (e.g. £), and the restatement in purchasing power units (e.g. $£_g$). For purposes of adjustment, however, monetary resources and liabilities are left at their face value; non-monetary assets not already expressed in current purchasing power terms are restated in these terms; so, too, is the opening capital or residual equity; and, to keep the identity in balance, the periodic purchasing power loss caused by holding monetary resources, and the equivalent purchasing power gain resulting from having borrowed money, are both recognized. Any transactions (monetary or non-monetary) during the period would have required some adjustment using an inflation factor of some fraction of p (depending on when they took place during the year).

The above notation raises an interesting issue which has been the cause of a great deal of debate in recent years – i.e. the question of the purchasing power losses and gains of $M_t p$ and $L_t p$. The former represents an estimate of the loss in purchasing power suffered by the entity because it has held monetary assets (such as cash and debtors) during a period of inflation – in other words, the effect of inflation will have been to reduce the purchasing power of such resources during the period in which they were held. As such, it represents a form of depreciation (i.e. not of a money value fall, but because of the fall in the value of money). The factor of $L_tp$, in contrast, represents a notional purchasing power gain to the entity at the expense of its borrowers. By lending it money during a period of inflation, it is assumed that the borrowers lose this purchasing power during the period of borrowing (and, correspondingly, the entity becomes the beneficiary).

Both these inflationary data arise out of the price-level restatement process, but both should be reasonably familiar to those who have experienced inflation: they represent commonly held 'inflationary' attitudes (i.e. spend rather than save cash because it loses purchasing power; and borrow as much as possible and repay later in units of diminished purchasing power). However, there is a growing debate as to the accounting validity and meaning of these monetary gains and losses.[3] In particular, the main question is whether or not they are elements of income, and opinions vary on their accounting. To the extent that they are representative of increases or decreases in purchasing power (as distinct from money), and opening capital is being maintained in current purchasing power terms, it is feasible to classify them as such (they represent changes in the purchasing power of the entity's capital). On the other hand, if capital is being maintained in terms either of money, operating capacity, command over alternative goods and services, or value to the business, it has to be asked whether $M_tp$ and $L_tp$ are representative of anything substantive.

For purposes of resolving this problem, it can be argued that $M_tp$ and $L_tp$ ought to be examined separately. First, so far as the loss in monetary assets is concerned, it appears that the loss in purchasing power to the business because it has such holdings will result eventually in the need for additional finance when these resources are used for operational activity. Therefore, it would appear to be prudent to make proper provision for such monetary depreciation when determining periodic income (in order that capital be maintained and unless the resources are permanently surplus to requirements). Secondly, the gain on holding borrowings during a period of inflation is more problematic. It is not clear that such a gain is anything other than an anomaly of the book-keeping process which creates it. Unlike any other unrealized gain in accounting, it does not result eventually in an additional cash input to the business entity. Consequently, the argument for excluding it from income is reasonably strong. However, the illustration in this chapter will follow the usually recommended professional practice of treating them as income elements, thereby making them compatible with these recommendations.

The above notation is a conceptual introduction to the process of restating opening accounting capital (R) so as to maintain capital in the same purchasing terms when determining periodic traditional accounting income based on historic cost. Illustration 23 describes the practical effect of this process, using the figures already used in most of the previous illustrations of traditional accounting and current value

**Table 5**

*(a) Income statements*

| | Period | | | |
|---|---|---|---|---|
| | $t_0-t_1$ £ | $t_1-t_2$ £ | $t_2-t_3$ £ | $t_3-t_4$ £ |
| Operational income before depreciation | 2,000 | 2,500 | 1,700 | — |
| *Less:* depreciation | 300 | 300 | 300 | 200 |
| | 1,700 | 2,200 | 1,400 | (200) |
| *Add:* capital gain | — | — | — | 5,300 |
| *Accounting income* | 1,700 | 2,200 | 1,400 | 5,100 |

*(b) Balance sheets*

| | Time | | | |
|---|---|---|---|---|
| | $t_1$ £ | $t_2$ £ | $t_3$ £ | $t_4$ £ |
| Shop | 5,000 | 5,000 | 5,000 | — |
| Van | 900 | 600 | 300 | — |
| Cash | 2,000 | 4,500 | 6,200 | — |
| | 7,900 | 10,100 | 11,500 | — |
| Capital | 6,200 | 6,200 | 6,200 | — |
| Retained income of prior periods | — | 1,700 | 3,900 | — |
| Retained income of current period | 1,700 | 2,200 | 1,400 | — |
| | 7,900 | 10,100 | 11,500 | — |

**Illustration 23   Price-level restated accounting income**

(a) *Income statements restated*

| | Period | | | |
|---|---|---|---|---|
| | $t_0-t_1$ £g | $t_1-t_2$ £g | $t_2-t_3$ £g | $t_3-t_4$ £g |
| Operational income before depreciation | 2,095[a] | 2,619[b] | 1,780[c] | — |
| *Less:* depreciation | 330[d] | 363[e] | 399[f] | 328[g] |
| | 1,765 | 2,256 | 1,381 | (328) |
| *Add:* capital gain | — | — | — | 4,007[h] |
| | 1,765 | 2,256 | 1,381 | 3,679 |
| *Less:* loss on holding cash | 95[i] | 319[j] | 526[k] | — |
| *Restated accounting income* | 1,670 | 1,937 | 855 | 3,679 |

(b) *Balance sheets restated*

| | Time | | | |
|---|---|---|---|---|
| | $t_1$ £g | $t_2$ £g | $t_3$ £g | $t_4$ £g |
| Shop | 5,500[m] | 6,050[n] | 6,650[o] | — |
| Van | 990[p] | 726[q] | 399[r] | — |
| Cash | 2,000 | 4,500 | 6,200 | — |
| | 8,490 | 11,276 | 13,249 | — |
| Capital | 6,820[s] | 7,502[t] | 8,246[u] | —[v] |
| Retained income of prior periods | — | 1,837[w] | 4,148[x] | —[y] |
| Retained income of current period | 1,670 | 1,937 | 855 | —[z] |
| | 8,490 | 11,276 | 13,249 | — |

(a) £2,000×110/105; (b) £2,500×121/115·5; (c) £1,700×133/127;
(d) £300×110/100; (e) £300×121/100; (f) £300×133/100;
(g) £300×146/100−£100×146/133; (h) £10,300×146/133−£5,000×146/100;
(i) £2,000×110/105−£2,000; (j) (£2,000×121/110+£2,500×121/115·5)−£4,500;
(k) (£4,500×133/121+£1,700×133/127)−£6,200; (l) £16,600×146/133−£16,600;
(m) £5,000×110/100; (n) £5,000×121/100; (o) £5,000×133/100;
(p) £900×110/100; (q) £600×121/100; (r) £300×133/100; (s) £6,200×110/100;
(t) £6,200×121/100; (u) £6,200×133/100; (v) £6,200×146/100−£6,200×146/100;
(w) £g1,670×121/110; (x) £g3,774×133/121;
(y) £g5,003×146/133−£g5,003×146/133; (z) £g3,679−3,679.

incomes. Illustration 23 takes the traditional accounting income and balance sheet figures used in Chapter 4, Illustration 12 (page 50), as in Table 5. It restates each of the above income statements and balance sheets in current purchasing power terms existing at each period end, assuming the general price index at $t_0$ to be 100, at $t_1$ 110, at $t_2$ 121, at $t_3$ 133, and at $t_4$ 146 – i.e. an approximate 10 per cent increase in prices during each period. The above figures are subject to the situation and assumptions described previously in Illustration 12.

The complexity of the calculations in the illustration demands some further explanation:

*1 Operational income:* These measures have been assumed to have been earned evenly throughout the periods concerned. Therefore, in order to restate them in money values existing at the end of each period, an average periodic index of the general price movement has been applied,

$$\text{e.g. } 110 / \ \frac{110+100}{2} \ \text{ or } \ \frac{110}{105} \ \text{ in period } t_0 - t_1.$$

This is intended to recognize that some of the income was earned at the beginning of the period (thus requiring a full period's index adjustment) and some at the end (requiring no restatement whatsoever).

*2 Depreciation:* Periodic depreciation in the first three periods has been computed on a straight-line basis of 25 per cent of the original cost of £1,200 at $t_0$. In order for the various charges to be re-expressed in money terms at $t_1$, $t_2$ and $t_3$, indices reflecting price movements since $t_0$ must be applied in each case, i.e. using a base of 100. During the last period, there is a loss on realization of £200 (£300 – 100) in historic cost terms which has been treated as an operating loss. To restate this in terms of money values at $t_4$, the £300 book value (in terms of $t_0$ money values) and the £100 sale proceeds (in terms of $t_3$ money values) must have appropriate indices of price movements applied to them, i.e. 146/100 and 146/133, respectively.

*3 Capital gain:* The gain on the sale of the shop is an unadjusted £10,300 – 5,000 or £5,300. To express it in terms of money values at $t_4$, the proceeds of £10,300 received just after $t_3$ will have an index of price movement for $t_3 - t_4$ applied (146/133); and the original cost of £5,000 paid at $t_0$ will have an index of price movement for $t_0 - t_4$ applied (146/100).

*4 Loss on holding cash:* In accordance with the conceptual identity described on pages 136–8, if monetary resources are held for any period of time when prices in general are rising, a monetary loss must be accounted for if the process of restatement is to be complete. The computation of the periodic loss, as the above workings show, is normally of two parts: first, the conversion of the opening balances allowing for a full period's price movement; and secondly, the conversion of monetary resources created by operational income of the period (this will be converted using the same average index as was applied to operational income). The difference between the restated monetary resources and their face value is the required loss in generalized purchasing power terms.

*Note*: Categories (1) to (4) of adjustment give restated historic cost based income figures which are then incorporated in the appropriate balance sheets.

*5 Shop:* The shop was purchased at $t_0$ when the general price index stood at 100. Therefore, at each subsequent point in time, its historic cost needs to be restated in the money value terms then pertaining.

*6 Van:* A similar exercise to that concerning the shop must be conducted for the van; the only difference is that it is the undepreciated portion of the historic cost which requires adjustment.

*7 Capital:* The original capital of £6,200 at $t_0$ is periodically adjusted into current purchasing power terms by the application of a periodic index using a $t_0$ base of 100, the time when capital is assumed to have been originally subscribed. Note (v) reflects the closing adjustment (in terms of purchasing power at $t_4$) immediately after $t_3$ when business operations ceased.

*8 Retained income of prior periods:* The retained earnings of previous periods are readjusted continuously into current money value terms by the application of the appropriate period index, thus completing the process of restating total opening capital. The cessation of business operations immediately after $t_3$ is described in note (y) with the final distribution of retained income in $t_4$ purchasing power terms.

*9 Retained income of current period:* This is the balancing figure which has been already computed in stages (1) to (4) inclusive. When expressed in terms of purchasing power at $t_4$, it is removed from the accounting records because of the cessation immediately after $t_3$ (note (z)).

The above computations form the essential elements in translating historic cost income data into contemporary money value terms. It should not, however, be mistaken as a current valuation process. The value base still remains historic cost, and the measurement unit is simply a restated historic cost. It is a process of updating the measurement unit to eliminate the effect of fluctuating money values. In this respect, the process is akin to that involved when converting foreign currencies into a common currency for financial reporting purposes. It does not therefore alleviate any of the problems inherent in the traditional accounting model and brought about by relatively strict adherence to the realization principle. Current values and holding gains are not recognized in the basic model, nor in its restated form. Its main aim is essentially to maintain the capital of the proprietors of the entity in current purchasing power terms so that, should the entity be liquidated, the capital returned will have the same purchasing power as that subscribed originally and retained subsequently.

Grave doubts must also remain as to the meaning of the adjusted historic cost figures. There are the questions of the suitability of the general price index applied (this will be dealt with separately on pages 154–5); the assumption of averaging in the accrual of income and monetary resources during the year (how accurate can this ever be as an assumption?); and the fact that the adjusted data represent neither the factual values from which it originated nor any current values to which it may be presently related (except by accident). The restated figures therefore appear to be representative of nothing very conclusive, and, since they could be mistaken for current values, they may be said to be potentially misleading. On the whole, it cannot be said to be a particularly useful or relevant process owing to the fact that it leaves accounting income still measured on the basis of the principles of historic cost and realization.

### Restatement of current value income

Because price-level restatement is a monetary adjusting process, applicable to all income models, a series of adjustments similar to those described in the previous section can be applied to current value income (in both its entry and exit value forms). The purpose of such adjustments is, however, not only to account for monetary gains and losses, but also, more significantly, to segregate those parts of the various operational and holding gains which are inflationary, owing to a general movement in prices, from those which are real, owing to a relative movement in prices; i.e. to maintain the real capital value of the entity. This may be conceptually described as follows, using the same situation, assumptions and notation already used in the preceding section:

> Assume that $M_t + N_t = R_t + L_t$; and that there are no operational or capital receipt and repayment transactions during the defined period t to t+1. Assume also that s is the specific price movement during the period, applicable to non-monetary resources. Then at t+1, by applying this specific price change, the restated identity would be $M_t + N_t(1+s) = R_t + L_t + N_t s$; where $N_t s$ represents the specific non-monetary holding gain.

This is equivalent, in a most basic form, to the current value computations described in Chapters 5, 6, 7 and 8 – i.e. the recognition of specific price changes (either entry or exit) with the supporting assumption of monetary stability. However, if it is also assumed that the general movement in prices during the same period is p, then it is possible to restate the above specific price restatement identity as a relative price identity:

> First, by taking the basic identity of $M_t + N_t = R_t + L_t$ and applying the general price factor throughout, the restated identity becomes:
>
> $$M_t(1+p) + N_t(1+p) = R_t(1+p) + L_t(1+p); \text{ thus}$$
>
> $$M_t + M_t p + N_t + N_t p = R_t + R_t p + L_t + L_t p$$
>
> Subtracting the unadjusted identity of $M_t + N_t = R_t + L_t$ from the above, the following residue remains:
>
> $$M_t p + N_t p = R_t p + L_t p; \text{ or } R_t p + L_t p - M_t p - N_t p = O$$

This latest identity may be added to the right-hand side of the specific price identity derived above, i.e.

$$M_t + N_t(1+s) = R_t + L_t + N_t s + R_t p + L_t p - M_t p - N_t p$$
$$= R_t(1+p) + L_t + N_t(s-p) + L_t p - M_t p.$$

In other words, by restating non-monetary resources in specific current price terms, and by restating residual equity using the general price index, it becomes necessary to recognize the monetary purchasing power loss ($M_t p$) and the equivalent gain on liabilities ($L_t p$), leaving the specific holding gain on non-monetary resources expressed in relative price terms ($N_t(s-p)$) – the initial identity expressed in money (£) terms but the final identity being restated in purchasing power ($£_g$) terms. It is the latter identity which is followed in practice when computing business and realizable incomes in relative terms. (It

**Table 6**

*(a) Income statements*

| | Period | | | |
|---|---|---|---|---|
| | $t_0-t_1$ £ | $t_1-t_2$ £ | $t_2-t_3$ £ | $t_3-t_4$ £ |
| Current operating profit | 1,650 | 2,075 | 1,250 | (350) |
| Realized cost savings of period | 50 | 75 | 25 | — |
| Unrealized cost savings of period | 150 | 150 | 25 | — |
| Realized capital gains of period | — | — | — | 300 |
| Unrealized capital gains of period | 1,000 | 1,500 | 2,500 | — |
| *Business income* | 2,850 | 3,800 | 3,800 | (50) |

*(b) Balance sheets*

| | Time | | | |
|---|---|---|---|---|
| | $t_1$ £ | $t_2$ £ | $t_3$ £ | $t_4$ £ |
| Shop | 6,000 | 7,500 | 10,000 | — |
| Van | 1,050 | 850 | 450 | — |
| Cash | 2,000 | 4,500 | 6,200 | — |
| | 9,050 | 12,850 | 16,650 | — |
| Capital | 6,200 | 6,200 | 6,200 | — |
| Retained income of prior periods | — | 2,850 | 6,650 | — |
| Retained income of current period | 2,850 | 3,800 | 3,800 | — |
| | 9,050 | 12,850 | 16,650 | — |

*(c)* The general price movements assumed in Illustration 23 are also assumed in Illustrations 24 and 25.

is not intended to restate current cost income because the procedures are identical to those applied to business and realizable incomes. The remainder of this chapter will therefore deal only with the adjustments to replacement cost and net realizable value data. The following illustrations describe this: Illustration 24 on restated business income using the unadjusted data derived in Chapter 6, Illustration 15 (pages 79ff.), and Illustration 25 on restated realizable income using the unadjusted data in Chapter 7, Illustration 16 (pages 95–6). The unadjusted business income statements and balance sheets are as in Table 6.

As with the restatement of the traditional accounting income model (pages 139–42), price-level calculations in Illustration 24 are not particularly easy to follow. However, they do adhere to the pattern laid out in the conceptual identity already derived in this section, i.e. $M_t + N_t(1+s) = R_t(1+p) + L_t + N_t(s-p) + L_tp - M_tp$; allowing for the fact that there are no liabilities in the above example. The resources side of the balance sheet identity is expressed already in specific price terms (replacement costs) and, therefore, needs no further adjustment. On the other hand, the capital side of the identity does require restatement: equity capital is re-expressed in terms of current monetary values, as is retained income of prior periods; whereas income of the period is re-expressed to eliminate the inflationary element from realized and unrealized holding gains, and to recognize the loss on holding cash when prices are rising in general. The following additional comments are given to support the detail of the workings. The reader should become familiar with the specific price movements pertaining to this example, which were given in detail in Illustration 15 (pages 79 ff.).

1 *Current operating profits:* The operational cash surplus, assumed throughout to accrue evenly during each period, has been restated in terms of current purchasing power at each period end by applying an appropriate average index of price movement for the period. This is similar to the adjustment made to traditional accounting income. Depreciation, because it is already expressed in current price terms, does not require further adjustment. It should be noted that this restatement of current operating profit is contrary to the treatment usually advocated by the supporters of the restated business income model. They assume such income elements are already expressed in current purchasing power terms, and therefore do not require adjustment. This assumption does not appear to be valid, however, since

**Illustration 24 Price-level restated business income**

*(a) Income statements restated*

| | Period | | | |
|---|---|---|---|---|
| | $t_0-t_1$ $£_g$ | $t_1-t_2$ $£_g$ | $t_2-t_3$ $£_g$ | $t_3-t_4$ $£_g$ |
| Current operating profit | 1,745[a] | 2,194[b] | 1,330[c] | (384)[d] |
| Realized cost savings of period | 20[e] | 40[f] | (17)[g] | — |
| Unrealized cost savings of period | 60[h] | 80[i] | (17)[j] | — |
| Realized capital gains of period | — | — | — | 329[k] |
| Unrealized capital gains of period | 500[l] | 900[m] | 1,756[n] | — |
| | 2,325 | 3,214 | 3,052 | (55) |
| *Less:* loss on holding cash | 95[o] | 319[o] | 526[o] | —[o] |
| *Restated business income* | 2,230 | 2,895 | 2,526 | (55) |

*(b) Balance sheets restated*

| | Time | | | |
|---|---|---|---|---|
| | $t_1$ $£_g$ | $t_2$ $£_g$ | $t_3$ $£_g$ | $t_4$ $£_g$ |
| Shop | 6,000 | 7,500 | 10,000 | — |
| Van | 1,050 | 850 | 450 | — |
| Cash | 2,000 | 4,500 | 6,200 | — |
| | 9,050 | 12,850 | 16,650 | — |
| Capital | 6,820[p] | 7,502[q] | 8,246[r] | —[s] |
| Retained income of prior periods | — | 2,453[t] | 5,878[u] | —[v] |
| Retained income of current period | 2,230 | 2,895 | 2,526 | —[w] |
| | 9,050 | 12,850 | 16,650 | — |

(a) £2,000×110/105−£350; (b) £2,500×121/115·5−£425;
(c) £1,700×133/127−£450; (d) £100×146/133−£450×146/133;
(e) £50−½×10/100×£1,200; (f) £75−½×11/110×£1,400;
(g) £25−½×12/121×£1,700; (h) £150−¾×10/100×£1,200;
(i) £150−½×11/110×£1,400; (j) £25−½×12/121×£1,700;
(k) £10,300×146/133−£10,000×146/133; (l) £1,000−10/100×£5,000;
(m) £1,500−11/110×£6,000; (n) £2,500−12/121×£7,500; (o) these calculations are
identical to those given in notes (i) (j) (k) and (l) of Illustration 23;
(p) £6,200×110/100; (q) £6,200×121/100; (r) £6,200×133/100;
(s) £6,200×146/100−£6,200×146/100; (t) $£_g$2,230×121/110; (u) $£_g$5,348×133/121;
(v) $£_g$8,404×146/133−$£_g$8,404×146/133; (w) $£_g$(55)−(55).

operating surpluses do not arise solely at the end of each relevant period. The loss on realization of the van, which occurred just after point $t_3$, has to be restated in terms of money values at $t_4$ – hence the application of the appropriate general price index for period $t_3-t_4$ to the undepreciated replacement cost balance of £450 and the sale proceeds of £100 (see working note (d)).

*2 Realized and unrealized cost savings:* These specific price holding gains, which arise from increases in the replacement cost of a depreciable resource, and which are realized through writing off replacement cost depreciation, are readjusted to eliminate the general price gain, thereby leaving the relative price gain. For example, taking working note (e), the specific price gain of £50 contains an inflationary element which would have amounted to one-quarter (a proportion equivalent to the fraction of the resource's replacement cost being written off) of the gain found by applying that period's general price movement (10 per cent) to the opening replacement cost of the van (£1,200). Likewise, taking working note (h), the unrealized specific price gain of £150, so far not written off by way of depreciation, is compared with the equivalent general price gain which is based upon the opening replacement cost of £1,200 (i.e. three-quarters of 10 per cent of £1,200).

*3 Realized and unrealized capital gains:* A similar process to that described for cost savings is conducted for unrealized capital gains: i.e. applying the general price movement to the opening replacement cost and deducting the resultant inflationary gain from the specific price gain, thereby leaving the relative price gain. So far as the realized capital gain is concerned, it occurred just after $t_3$ and, like the loss on realization of the van, needs to be re-expressed in terms of money values at $t_4$.

*4 Other items:* The computation of the figures relating to losses from holding cash and to capital and retained income of prior periods is identical in principle to those previously described in the restated traditional accounting income model.

The unadjusted realizable income statements and balance sheets are as in Table 7, and are subject to the value increases described in Illustration 16 (pages 95–6), and the general price movements described in Illustration 23 (page 139).

**Table 7**

*(a) Income statements*

| | Period | | | |
|---|---|---|---|---|
| | $t_0-t_1$ £ | $t_1-t_2$ £ | $t_2-t_3$ £ | $t_3-t_4$ £ |
| Operating gains | 2,000 | 2,500 | 1,700 | — |
| Unrealized non-operating gains (losses) of the period: van | (350) | (500) | (250) | — |
| shop | 700 | 1,300 | 2,500 | — |
| Realized non-operating gains of the period: shop | — | — | — | 800 |
| *Realizable income* | 2,350 | 3,300 | 3,950 | 800 |

*(b) Balance sheets*

| | Time | | | |
|---|---|---|---|---|
| | $t_1$ £ | $t_2$ £ | $t_3$ £ | $t_4$ £ |
| Shop | 5,700 | 7,000 | 9,500 | — |
| Van | 850 | 350 | 100 | — |
| Cash | 2,000 | 4,500 | 6,200 | — |
| | 8,550 | 11,850 | 15,800 | — |
| Capital | 6,200 | 6,200 | 6,200 | — |
| Retained income of prior periods | — | 2,350 | 5,650 | — |
| Retained income of current period | 2,350 | 3,300 | 3,950 | — |
| | 8,550 | 11,850 | 15,800 | — |

The adjustments described in Illustration 25 are identical in principle to those related to the restated business income model: that is, the restatement of operating gains by adjusting the periodic cash surpluses by appropriate average general price indices; the elimination of the inflationary elements from the various realized and unrealized holding gains and losses; the incorporation in the restated income statements of the periodic purchasing power losses due to holding cash resources;

**Illustration 25  Price-level restated realizable income**

*(a) Income statements restated*

|  | Period | | | |
| --- | --- | --- | --- | --- |
|  | $t_0-t_1$ $£_g$ | $t_1-t_2$ $£_g$ | $t_2-t_3$ $£_g$ | $t_3-t_4$ $£_g$ |
| Operating gains | 2,095[a] | 2,619[b] | 1,780[c] | — |
| Unrealized non-operating gains (losses) of period: van | (470)[d] | (585)[e] | (285)[f] | — |
| shop | 200[g] | 730[h] | 1,806[i] | — |
| Realized non-operating gains of period: shop | — | — | — | 878[j] |
|  | 1,825 | 2,764 | 3,301 | 878 |
| *Less:* loss on holding cash | 95[k] | 319[k] | 526[k] | —[k] |
| *Restated realizable income* | 1,730 | 2,445 | 2,775 | 878 |

*(b) Balance sheets restated*

|  | Time | | | |
| --- | --- | --- | --- | --- |
|  | $t_1$ $£_g$ | $t_2$ $£_g$ | $t_3$ $£_g$ | $t_4$ $£_g$ |
| Shop | 5,700 | 7,000 | 9,500 | — |
| Van | 850 | 350 | 100 | — |
| Cash | 2,000 | 4,500 | 6,200 | — |
|  | 8,550 | 11,850 | 15,800 | — |
| Capital | 6,820[l] | 7,502[l] | 8,246[l] | —[l] |
| Retained income of prior periods | — | 1,903[m] | 4,779[n] | —[o] |
| Retained income of current period | 1,730 | 2,445 | 2,775 | —[p] |
|  | 8,550 | 11,850 | 15,800 | — |

(a) £2,000×110/105; (b) £2,500×121/115·5; (c) £1,700×133/127;
(d) £(350+10/100×£1,200); (e) £(500+11/110×£850); (f) £(250+12/121×£350);
(g) £700−10/100×£5,000; (h) £1,300−11/110×£5,700; (i) £2,500−12/121×£7,000;
(j) £800×146/133; (k) these calculations are identical to those given in notes (i), (j), (k) and (l) of Illustration 23; (l) these calculations are identical to those given in notes (p), (q), (r) and (s) of Illustration 24; (m) $£_g$1,730×121/110; (n) $£_g$4,348×133/121;
(o) $£_g$7,554×146/133−$£_g$7,554×146/133; (p) $£_g$878−878.

the lack of adjustment to the resources part of the balance sheet which is already in current money value terms; and the periodic restatement by an annual general price index of the measures of opening capital and retained income of prior periods.

Before proceeding further, it is worthwhile noting the approach of Chambers[4] to general price-level accounting. It is very much simpler than above – involving only one adjustment in every period, a transfer from the income statement to a capital maintenance reserve. The figure transferred is the general index movement for the period applied to the opening current value capital (with this including aggregate retained income). It is intended to represent the periodic loss in generalized purchasing power in opening capital which requires to be provided for at the end of the period if opening current value

**Illustration 26  Chambers' purchasing power adjustments**

|  | Period | | | | |
|---|---|---|---|---|---|
|  | $t_0-t_1$ £ | $t_1-t_2$ £ | $t_2-t_3$ £ | $t_3-t_4$ £ | Total £ |
| Realizable income | 2,350 | 3,300 | 3,950 | 800 | 10,400 |
| *Less*: capital maintenance adjustments | 620[a] | 855[b] | 1,175[c] | —[d] | 2,650 |
| *Adjusted realizable income* | 1,730 | 2,445 | 2,775 | 800 | 7,740 |

|  | Time | | | | |
|---|---|---|---|---|---|
|  | $t_0$ £ | $t_1$ £ | $t_2$ £ | $t_3$ £ | $t_4$ £ |
| Capital | 6,200 | 6,200 | 6,200 | 6,200 | — |
| Retained income (adjusted) | — | 1,730 | 4,175[e] | 6,950[f] | — |
| Capital maintenance reserve | — | 620 | 1,475[g] | 2,650[h] | — |
| *Total assets* | 6,200 | 8,550 | 11,850 | 15,800 | — |

(a) £6,200×110/100−£6,200; (b) £8,550×121/110−£8,550;
(c) £11,850×133/121−£11,850; (d) no adjustment needed because of cessation of business immediately after $t_3$; (e) £1,730+2,445; (f) £4,175+2,775; (g) £620+855; (h) £1,475+1,175.

capital is to be maintained in purchasing power terms. Using the total realizable income and capital figures in Table 7, and applying the general index movements used throughout this chapter, Illustration 26 outlines the adjustments recommended by Chambers.

## Price-level restatement and current value accounting

Earlier chapters, as well as earlier sections of this chapter, have treated price-level restatement and current value accounting as separate topics. This has been done deliberately since they are separate issues and functions. However, because current value accounting is, in fact, recognizing price-level changes and movements, there is some confusion about the differences between general price-level changes, specific price-level changes, and current values. The purpose of this section is to attempt a clarification.

The aim of general price-level restatement, as described in this chapter, is to revalue the monetary measurement unit used in the process of determining periodic income. By restating opening capital in the way described above, income is determined by comparing opening and closing capital measured in the same general purchasing power terms. Price-level restatement is therefore part of the process of capital maintenance. Current value accounting, on the other hand, is, as the term suggests, a valuation process necessary to determine capital for capital maintenance and income determination purposes. It is therefore a distinctly different function from that of price-level restatement.

A further source of misunderstanding in this area is that specific price indices exist for particular goods or services, or for particular industries or types of business. In fact, it is perfectly feasible for a specific index to be compiled which is representative of the monetary purchasing pattern of a particular individual or business entity. These specific indices are, however, averages of particular market prices for particular goods and services, and should therefore be distinguished from current values (whether exit or entry) which are based on individual market prices. A specific price index could therefore be used as a surrogate for a current value when market prices cannot be obtained directly; or, when such an index represents the purchasing power of an individual or an entity, it could be used as a form of general index to apply in the process of price-level restatement. Specific price indices can therefore be used in both the valuation process and the capital maintenance process necessary to income determination; but such usage constitutes two separate functions.

## Advantages of price-level restatement

The process of price-level restatement has been described in some detail. It therefore now seems appropriate to comment on both its main advantages and attendant disadvantages. The advantages are listed first.

To start with, it attempts to alleviate the problem of determining income with a measuring unit which has a variable value. It is intended, through the technique of adjusting opening capital, to maintain capital in the same general purchasing power terms. Its main advantage, therefore, is that it segregates those elements of periodic value increments which do not represent a factual increase in entity resources from those which do.

Secondly, price-level restatement, by eliminating inflationary gains and losses, gives additional information to the user of financial statements which may very well provide him with a better base on which to found his predictions relating to future entity progress.

Thirdly, the process of price-level restatement is a constant, an optional extra, which may be applied to any of the main accounting and economic models of income. It therefore has a commendable universality common to them all, and one which does not interfere with the various fundamental valuation and capital maintenance functions which have to be conducted before restatement takes place.

Fourthly, because the process attempts to give the entire income determination function a comparable common denominator in the form of a 'stabilized' monetary unit, it has been suggested that this provides accounting data about an entity's economic progress and position which are more comparable, both inter- and intra- firm, than unadjusted data. Such comparability, however, can only be achieved if the restated data are continuously updated into contemporary purchasing power terms. In this sense, price-level restatement is not a once-and-for-all process. Summaries of several years' data for comparative purposes would therefore need considerable and continuous readjustment: a process which necessarily was conducted with the economic examples but which has not been attempted in the accounting examples in this chapter (each year being treated on its own merits).

Fifthly, the time and cost factors involved in producing price-level restated accounting information are not excessive. It is a process which can be undertaken after the basic income and capital computations have been made, at little extra expense, provided the underlying accounting records are adequately and timeously maintained.

There are several counter-arguments to the five arguments listed above, most of which dismiss the usefulness of price-level restated income in any of its forms.

First, it has been argued that, since the restatement process is intended to express opening and closing capital in the same generalized purchasing power, this itself invalidates it: i.e. generalized purchasing power has no relevance to any person or entity because no such thing exists in reality, except as a statistician's computation. Such statistical averages normally bear no relationship to the specific purchasing pattern and structure of a particular entity, and are therefore said to be meaningless appendages to the income determination function. This, it should be noted, is not an argument against price-level restatement *per se*. It is more an argument for the use in such a process of specific generalized price indices which correspond with the monetary purchasing power of particular entities.

Secondly, and following on from this first point, there is the argument that the price indices used in these calculations, no matter how relevant a particular entity, are only statistical averages. They cannot include the prices negotiated in every transaction during the specified period, and so, to that extent, are less than perfect indicators of price movements. In addition, they are usually domestic or household consumer averages, and do not reflect prices relevant to manufacturing or trading entities.

Thirdly, the question of the meaning of the restated accounting data is a focal point for much of the discontent with the restatement process. This is particularly so in connection with the restatement of historic cost data, and, especially, the adjustment of the various resource costs, which, once undertaken, result in figures which are neither the original ones transacted nor current valuations of these resources. In the same way, it can be said that the restatements of current value models have limited meaning since they lead to a re-allocation of the various capital and retained income elements in the appropriate current value balance sheets. In this respect, price-level restatement is simply a function of how capital and capital maintenance is perceived; it does not alter the fundamental factors of segregating realized from unrealized gains, or operating from holding gains. In particular, if holding gains are regarded as capital adjustments rather than as income (as in the operating capacity concept of business income), then price-level restatement does not add much information to the model apart from the computation of monetary losses and gains (which could be computed without going through the entire elaborate procedure of restatement).

Fourthly, it has been argued that the problem of fluctuating money values is not one which is relevant to the accountant, and that he should not have to cope with a matter which is the concern of the economist or the statistician. In this respect, it is also argued that, by making these adjustments, the accountant is hiding the reality of the basic recorded data.

## The index problem

The problem of which price index to apply to the various income models is a vexed and long-standing one. There are, in fact, several to choose from. There is the concept of generalized purchasing power, as expressed in the Consumer Price Index or the Index of Retail Prices: both of these refer to consumer domestic prices and are based on statistical averages derived from a rather limited 'typical' housewife's shopping basket, the consumer index being more representative but less available than the retail one. There are therefore doubts as to whether this type of index has sufficient relevance to the purchasing pattern and structure of an individual entity to be of use in price-level restatement. That they are used for such a purpose is a result of two factors: first, that they happen to be the only available official statistics of general price movements over defined periods; and secondly, that they reflect price movements which are more relevant to the proprietor of the entity than the entity itself (remembering that the original conception of restating traditional accounting income was to maintain the purchasing power of the proprietor as expressed in his capital). If the aim is to maintain the generalized purchasing power of the entity, however, the relevance of such consumer indices must be limited because of obvious variations in the particular purchasing patterns of individual entities. There are other indices in existence which should also be noted. There are, for example, specific indices for particular goods and services, or for particular industries. Because of their specific nature, however, these are not very good indicators of changes in the purchasing power of money – the very factor with which the process of price-level restatement is trying to cope. There are also specific indices of share prices, such as the Dow Jones or Financial Times Indices, which suffer from the previously mentioned defect, and which, in any case, have doubtful relevance to the individual entity.

The fundamental question arising from the above comments is really that of whether the capital to be maintained is to be perceived as that of the entity or that of its proprietor. It would seem logical to assume that it must be that of the entity, first, because the previous explanations of income determination have assumed an entity concept for income, value and capital, and secondly, because proprietorship tends to be less permanent than the entity in which the investment has been made—particularly, in limited companies. It would therefore be ideal to use a general index which reflected the change in monetary purchasing power affecting a particular entity, rather than an index which is so general that it could well be irrelevant to every person and every entity. For this reason, the solution would seem to be to construct a 'specific' general index related to a particular company and its pattern of prices over defined periods. To construct such an index, however, could be a somewhat forbidding task for a large and complex organization. It does nevertheless seem to be a logical suggestion, in view of the fact that the general price indices existing at present are arguably too general to be relevant to a particular entity, while the specific indices existing are arguably too narrow to be representative of changes in money values. Gynther[5] has tended to argue along these lines in stating that there is no such thing as generalized purchasing power, but that, rather, there exist many specific purchasing powers relevant to particular individuals and entities. Edwards and Bell[6] as well as Sterling,[7] on the other hand, take the opposite view that there is such a general monetary concept, and that the present limited consumer-based indices should be used because they are the best presently available. Until such time as 'specific' general indices can be constructed, the latter view appears the more practical if monetary restatement is felt to be desirable.

## The appropriateness of price-level restatement

Apart from the problem of the appropriateness of the general price index for use in the restatement process, there is the more fundamental problem of whether or not the process itself has relevance and meaning in the determination of income. Some writers argue for it; some against it; and, as yet, there is no general consensus of opinion. Some accountants have lent support to the general price adjustment of historic cost data while rejecting the reporting of specific price changes.[8] Economists[9] have argued for computations of 'real' income. The current value advocates[10] have also argued for restatement. These advocations have mainly been based on the grounds of the seriousness of the economic problem of inflation and its effect on money values over time. Gynther,[11] on the other hand, has argued that there is no such thing as a standard or stabilized monetary measuring unit; that there is no such thing as general purchasing power; that money does not have a general value; and that, because of these factors, general price-level restatement does not deal with the specific money problems of a particular entity; does not properly maintain the specific purchasing power of that entity; does not aid comparisons of specific entities; and clouds the reality of the entity's affairs which is necessary to the stewardship function. His argument follows the issue mentioned earlier of whether to maintain entity or proprietorship capital. As the former appears to be the most relevant concept in entity income determination, it would seem that Gynther's point has great validity.

Despite these obviously conflicting viewpoints, several factors should be emphasized at this stage. First, it is probable that restated data will increase the problems of comprehension facing the user of financial statements. Secondly, there do exist, as previously mentioned, serious and rational doubts about the meaning of many of the adjusted figures (particularly in the traditional accounting income model). Thirdly, there does not seem to be any wholly suitable general price index available which is universal to all entities (which thus creates doubts about the relevance of the restated data). And fourthly, most informed people would recognize and accept that there is a monetary problem caused by inflation which does have a bearing on the reported income and value data. It could therefore be suggested that general price-level changes should be recognized, not in the process of measuring income, but, instead, in the use of the relevant information. The onus would then be on the user to restate the data appropriately according to his or her purchasing pattern, rather than to leave the problem to the accountant. This, of course, follows the proprietorship concept, but completely ignores the entity concept, and looks like an abandonment of a relevant part of the capital maintenance process so necessary to the determination of entity income.

### References

(See pages 179–80 for Selected Bibliography

1. J. R. Hicks, *Value and Capital*, Clarendon Press, 1946, pp. 171–81 (reprinted as 'Income', in R. H. Parker and G. C. Harcourt (eds.), *Readings in the Concept and Measurement of Income*, Cambridge University Press, 1969, pp. 74–82, at p. 82).

2. I. Fisher, *The Theory of Interest*, Macmillan, 1930, pp. 3–35 (reprinted as 'Income and Capital', in Parker and Harcourt (eds.), op. cit., pp. 33–53, at pp. 37–9).

3. For example, J. R. Perrin, 'Illusory Holding Gains on Long-Term Debt', *Accounting and Business Research*, Summer 1974, pp. 234–6; M. Bourn, 'The "Gain" on Borrowing', *Journal of Business Finance and Accounting*, Spring 1976, pp. 167–82; D. Egginton and R. C. Morris, 'Holding Gains on Long-Term Liabilities: a Comment', *Accounting and Business Research*, Summer 1976, pp. 177–81; J. R. Grinyer, 'Holding Gains on Long-Term Liabilities: an Alternative Analysis', *Accounting and Business Research*, Spring 1978, pp. 130–48; and M. J. Mumford, 'Monetary Assets and Capital Gearing', *Journal of Business Finance and Accounting*, Autumn 1978, pp. 293–308.

4. R. J. Chambers, 'Accounting for Inflation', *Exposure Draft,* University of Sydney, 1975. This approach could be applied to any of the income models described in this text. It has the benefit of simplicity but, in the case of the historic cost model, the procedure suffers from the lack of prior accounting for unrealized specific price changes.

5. R. S. Gynther, 'Why Use General Purchasing Power?', *Accounting and Business Research,* Spring 1974, pp. 141−57.

6. E. O. Edwards and P. W. Bell, *The Theory and Measurement of Enterprise Income,* University of California Press, 1961, pp. 278−9.

7. R. R. Sterling, *Theory of the Measurement of Enterprise Income,* University of Kansas, 1970, pp. 339−41.

8. For example, R. Ma and M.C. Miller, 'Inflation and the Current Value Illusion', *Accounting and Business Research,* Autumn 1976, pp.250−63; P. Rosenfield, 'General Purchasing Power Acounting−Relevance and Interpretability', *Journal of Accountancy,* August 1975, pp.52−9; and P. Rosenfield, 'Current Replacement Value Accounting−a Dead End', *Journal of Accountancy,* September 1975, pp.63−73.

9. Hicks, op.cit., and Fisher, op.cit., in Parker and Harcourt (eds.), op.cit.

10. Edwards and Bell, *The Theory and Management of Enterprise Income;* and Sterling, *Theory of the Measurement of Enterprise Income.*

11. Gynther, 'Why Use General Purchasing Power?', op.cit.

# 11 The validity of the income concept

## Introduction

The object of this book has been to provide the reader with a reasonably detailed background to the main economic and accounting models of income in order to gain a relatively unprejudiced understanding of their nature and measurement. Thus far, the approach has been to present these matters in a hopefully unbiased manner so that the reader has not been hindered by the pursuit of an argument in favour of a single income model and in criticism of all others. The purpose, therefore, has not been to damn each model with faint praise but, instead, to allow the reader the freedom to learn and survey before entering the debate as to whether one income model is 'better' than any other; or, indeed, whether or not the concept of income is needed in practice. The time, however, has come to start asking questions of the concept, and this final chapter is therefore not merely an ending to this text; it is an opening to the income debate which the reader now joins; and it it is particularly a questioning of the income concept.

The validity of the income concept has been questioned by economists and accountants alike – despite its widespread use throughout several centuries. Hicks,[1] for example, whilst admitting that income has an important role to play as an influence on individual economic conduct, warned of the dangers of using it in economic argument; Frankel[2] also criticized it as a conventional symbol which can mask economic reality; and Solomons[3] considered it to be a concept which has been or will be superseded by information more relevant to decision making.

These, however, are minority views. As the earlier chapters in this text imply, the emphasis in recent years has been to expand rather than contract the theory and practice of income accounting. The utility of the various income models, nevertheless, is hard to assess – traditional accounting income has been evidenced in practice in a variety of uses over the years (for example, in investment, lending, wage negotiating, tax computations, and so on); but the alternative accounting models have not appeared sufficiently in practice to allow any substantial judgement to be made. All that can be said meantime from the available empirical research to date on these topics is that (a) the alternatives to traditional accounting income (particularly those using replacement costs and/or general price level adjustments) are regarded by both producers and users of financial information as potentially useful, but as a supplement to, rather than a substitute for, the historic cost model; (b) in time of inflation, the traditional accounting model seriously understates the income of the business entity when the latter is conceived in current value terms, and utilizes a physical resource notion of capital maintenance; and (c) all accounting alternatives to historic cost involve considerable computational and measurement problems, but none sufficiently so as to eliminate their consideration as practical alternatives to traditional accounting income. Despite this evidence, it therefore appears to be relevant at least to question the income concept on *a priori* grounds (irrespective of the different forms it may take), and the remaining sections of this text will attempt this. In doing so, they will also provide a brief summary of the main features of the income models described in earlier chapters.

## The elusive concept of income

The purpose of this section is to suggest that the income of a business entity is no more than a conventional financial management symbol which is capable of definition and computation in a variety of ways. In particular, the following points will be elaborated on:

**1** The problem of the existence of a variety of differing income concepts for reporting purposes because of different interpretations placed on the meaning of the underlying capital computations.

**2** The problem of flexibility with regard to the application of accounting principles in the process of income measurement.

**3** The problem of flexibility in accounting practice due to the degree of subjective judgement which is part of the income measurement process.

**4** The problem of unsatisfactory measures of income due to the exclusion of significant elements from the computation of capital, notably those relating to goodwill and other intangible resources.

## Differing concepts of income

As the earlier chapters in this text reveal, income cannot be thought of solely in terms of the traditional *ex post* periodic matchings of revenues from sales with related costs. Such may be the current concept of income, but it is certainly not the only one available. The economist's view of income, for example, is entirely different from that of matching past efforts and accomplishments. Conceived originally in terms of personal consumption and psychic experiences classified as enjoyment, its current form is based upon measures of periodic consumption plus periodic changes in the value of economic capital – the so-called concept of 'welloffness'. The economist uses these concepts of income as a means of theorizing about the economic behaviour of individuals, rather than of business entities. Consequently, they appear to be somewhat irrelevant to the business reporting function, which is concerned primarily with aggregate measures of entity activity. Enormous problems would arise in practice if any such adaptation to the accounting environment took place – e.g. forecasting over considerable periods of time, selecting an appropriate discount factor, the reinvestment constraint in order to maintain future 'welloffness', and the treatment and attribution of 'windfall' gains or losses.

Each of the above problems associated with the measurement of economic income tends to minimize the practical worth of the concept for financial reporting purposes. This is not to say that the various economic income models have no useful purpose – indeed they have, but only in the sense of helping to make rational theoretical explanations of income which aid an understanding of its nature – e.g. the rather false and misleading isolation of capital from income, as if they were two distinct and separate concepts, is avoided in the economic approach. Unfortunately, however, the practical problems mentioned above inevitably lead to an analysis of the alternative approaches to the accountant.

As previously mentioned, the traditional accounting approach to income measurement is an *ex post* one, involving a comparison of sales revenues with related costs through the so-called 'matching' process, and utilizing the realization principle. This process, whilst appearing eminently sensible, practical and objective, has several drawbacks. First, the basis of measuring transactions involving historic costs, together with the related realization principle, prevents the reporting of significant unrealized income elements, and results in the periodic reporting of a heterogeneous mixture of entity gains and losses; some relating to the current period and others to previous periods. If *ex post* measures of income are believed to be useful indicators of periodic business performance, both for control and predictive purposes, it can hardly be argued that the measures which are reported in the traditional model are particularly useful in these respects – income earned during the period concerned is not fully reported; contemporary values for all resources of the entity are not reported; and the reported income measure contains gains and losses earned in previous periods.

The imperfections of the traditional accounting income model have given rise, over the years, to a number of pleas for alternative accounting models which attempt to minimize its most obvious faults. These arguments have been mainly for the so-called current value models: where income is derived using current price-based values – i.e. either buying prices in terms of current replacement costs, selling prices in terms of current realizable values, or a mixture of both. Each of these models produce what can be radically different measures of income when using the same enterprise transactions. The differences arise because of the different value concepts which are applied to the measurement of capital. Nevertheless, each contains points of similarity which are worthy of note. They all abandon the traditional accounting principle of historic cost, because of the use of current valuations, and they ignore the restrictive realization principle. Thus, they present the realized and unrealized gains and losses of the defined period rather than a misleading mixture of income elements, as is the normal case with the traditional model. They also incorporate gains or losses resulting from operating activity as well as from the holding of resources.

As the foregoing remarks have indicated, each accounting model produces what can be significantly different measures of periodic income. This raises the question of what exactly is the income of the entity, and of which model provides the best indication of it. The historic cost model attempts to maintain the original money capital subscribed and retained in the enterprise; the replacement cost model involves maintenance of the physical resources underlying capital or of money capital (depending on which variant of the model is being used); the realizable value model involves maintenance of capital which could be invested in an alternative form; and the current cost model maintains value to the business. The problem with current value accounting, therefore, is that it adds several concepts to that already employed in practice, further complicating the issue of how best to report on entity activity.

The elusive nature of reportable enterprise income is further complicated by the relaxation of the traditional accounting measurement assumption of a stable monetary unit. If the reality of a monetary unit with a fluctuating value (in terms of its generalized purchasing power) is introduced into each of the aforementioned accounting models of income, then an equivalent number of further income models emerge – i.e. for each accounting model, there exists an adjusted and an unadjusted measure of income. (Adjusted in this sense means that the income measurement process has been undertaken allowing for changes in the generalized purchasing power of the monetary unit used.) The concept of income of the business entity cannot therefore be regarded as a straightforward issue; there are just too many variations to be considered, each raising the question of what exactly is the periodic income of an entity given a certain set of circumstances. As the earlier chapters in this text attempted to point out, however, each income model has its own role to play, and its own merits. As such, they are complementary rather than competing alternatives.

## Flexibility of accounting principles

The validity of the income concept as a useful part of the business reporting function is brought further into focus when the question of applying accounting principles in the measurement process is raised. In each of the historic cost and current value income models, the emphasis is entirely on entity performance, using measurements of known or forecast economic transactions. In order to construct these various measures, accountants have devised a series of measurement guidelines or principles which implement the process of allocation accounting so necessary to the periodic matching of revenues and costs – i.e. accounting principles related to such matters as the need to depreciate fixed assets; to provide for inventory of unsold stocks and work in progress; to defer taxation liabilities; to aggregate the financial results of a group of companies; to account for the consequences of a take-over or merger; and so on. However, whereas there can be a great deal of uniformity of meaning in these general principles, there is also a great deal of flexibility in their execution in practice (either in the historic cost framework or in its current value alternatives). This is no new problem; indeed, it has been recognized for a long time by accountants, and recently, at least within the context of the historic cost model, professional accountancy bodies throughout the world have commenced work on trying to narrow the areas of possible differences. This notwithstanding, it is inevitable that a significant degree of flexibility will remain (whatever the income model), which raises further doubts about the validity of a concept which is not only capable of differences in interpretation and measurement because of variations in capital and value concepts, but is also subject to differences due to an inevitable flexibility in measurement procedures.

## The problem of subjective judgement

There is one further aspect of accounting practice which arguably introduces the greatest degree of flexibility in income measurement. This relates to the application of subjective judgement by management and accountants during the income measurement process.

It is an inevitable aspect of financial accounting practice that the measurement process which is undertaken to derive periodic income contains a great deal of subjective judgement, particularly from the point of view of resource valuation. As a consequence, it is not unfair to suggest that subjective judgement, albeit of an expert and experienced kind, has a great deal of influence on the resultant capital and income measures. These personal judgements normally have to be made by experts in the appropriate area. However, such opinions are sought because of a lack of verifiable, objective evidence, and the possible variations in an opinion on a particular factor may thus be immense. The effect is to accentuate the possible flexibility in income measurement to extents which may cause income measures to be wide open to question because of doubts relating to the lack of objectivity exercised in their derivation. Thus, despite the laudable efforts of the professional accountancy bodies to minimize variety in accounting practice, it still remains a fact of life that no one can regulate against flexibility due to subjective judgement.

## Significant resource omission

In both accounting and economics, the relationship between income and capital is well established and accepted – one of the main differences between the approaches of the two disciplines being that the economist computes capital in order to derive income, whereas the accountant traditionally computes income, with capital being the residue of such an exercise. Whatever the approach, however, one point of similarity emerges – periodic income can be interpreted in terms of the periodic change in the value of capital. This means that, so far as income is concerned, it is important to ensure that capital is measured fully – i.e. that its value takes cognisance of all economic resources which contribute to the existence of income. However, if the historic cost and current value income models are examined, it is clearly seen that the relevant capital computations are incomplete, and that in most situations the capital of the business entity is computed on the basis of an aggregation of resource valuations which have arisen from past transactions and events. This means that significant business resources may well be omitted from the relevant capital and income computations, e.g. goodwill and other intangibles, which are often created rather than acquired by the entity.

The above comments lead to the apparent conclusion that the accounting models for determining periodic income are somewhat less than adequate because capital computations are incomplete. In addition, matchings of related sales and costs may result in overstated costs because of expenses incurred on the creation of goodwill being written off rather than capitalized (the former being the usual accounting practice).

## The meaning of income

If, as the evidence clearly suggests, income is a major part of economics and accounting, it is also clear that it should have some precise meaning, particularly for those persons who use it as part of their decision making and other activities. Surprisingly, despite its long history and the extent of its current use, the concept of income, as applied to the business entity, has remained ill defined, if it has been defined at all. Typically, in accounting, it is usually described in terms of an explanation of its measurement (i.e. as the difference between capital at two points of time; or as an increase in net wealth or owner's equity).

By way of contrast, economists are much more particular about the definition they use. Income has been described by them as a series of perceived events or psychic experiences called enjoyment, and as a means of giving individuals an indication of the amount which they can consume without impoverishing themselves. Thus, these approaches to income do not attempt to define it simply in terms of changes in càpital; they look at it in a much more fundamental way – as the so-called 'guide to prudent economic conduct'. As such it has been accepted by economists as the basis for analysing personal economic behaviour. In economics, therefore, the concept of income is no more than a man-made conventional symbol or indicator of economic conduct. It can therefore be adapted to the business entity in the familiar terms of financial prudence and the ultimate survival of the entity – i.e. as indicating the most appropriate consumption or distribution policy to be adopted if it is to survive and its owners are to be satisfied. However, despite the existence of economic definitions, it is evident that the meaning of income can be interpreted in a variety of ways.

First, income can be interpreted as the 'flow' of gains or benefits from a 'stock' of capital. This view of income is commonly adopted by accountants for purposes of differentiating between income and capital, particularly when establishing rates of return on capital, which can be used as indicators of the effective use made of the resources underlying capital. It arose presumably from the stewardship approach to financial reporting, where there is an evident need for management to account for the use of economic resources entrusted to it, as well as a need to determine the income and capital rights of individual owners or groups of owners, both when the entity is a going concern and when it is ultimately realized. However, there is a significant doubt regarding the meaningfulness of interpreting income as a 'flow' from a 'stock' of capital. Much depends on the classification for accounting purposes of expenditure which has ceased to have a useful service potential from that which still has.

Secondly, following on from the above point, it is evident that income of the business entity is believed to be indicative of the efficiency of management in connection with the holding and operational use made of the economic resources entrusted to it (i.e. in terms of returns on capital employed, etc.). But the term 'efficiency' is open to a variety of interpretations, depending on the attribute to which it refers – e.g. operational productivity, the quality of goods or services produced, the use made of machines or labour, or the effect of operations on the quality of the environment. 'Efficiency' also depends on the objectives which have been set for management – e.g. were these to produce a reasonable return on investment or to go all out to maximize the return? The question is therefore raised as to whether aggregate and periodic measures of income can be used to judge these complex matters (assuming, in any case, that the latter are made explicit). In addition, there is the possibility that managerial effectiveness and efficiency may well be being judged in the light of enterprise objectives which do not necessarily have a direct relationship to the traditional income objectives – i.e. social and economic considerations, such as the quality of life and the relationship of the entity to its socio-economic environment, can equally be regarded as important aspects of managerial behaviour.

Thirdly, reported income of the business entity is used by owners as an investment predictor – e.g. within the 'earnings per share' and 'price-earnings' measures which are specifically designed for this purpose. In other words, it may be presumed that the investment community finds measures of past income of use in predicting future income levels in order to predict the level of future distributions which, at least in part, determine investment values. Certainly, some knowledge of the past is useful when predicting the future, as it is the past and current situations which develop into those of the future. However, the volatility of business activity may well be an important factor in determining whether past income levels, and rates of change in these levels, are likely to persist in the future. In other words, it appears that, within the context of the meaning of income, income can be interpreted as a device of use in predicting future distribution levels, but that this implication has attendant disadvantages in the sense that the past need not necessarily repeat itself in the future. Given this uncertainty, it appears reasonable to question whether periodic income can be meaningful when used as a means of predicting the distributions to be made from the business entity to its owners.

### Information needs of investors and others

This section is concerned with what is arguably the most significant question to be asked of the concept of income as it relates to the business entity – i.e. are accounting measures of income relevant to the needs and requirements of those persons who use financial reports? For example, it must be concluded that measures of historic cost based income have been, and still are, assumed to be of use to owners and other persons interested in the affairs of entities, simply because of the past and current emphasis which is placed upon such measures in the function of financial reporting. But are they, or the alternative current value-based measures, of value to the persons who are assumed to use them?

It is a relatively self-evident observation that a variety of persons are interested, in varying degrees, in an individual entity and therefore require periodic information about its economic activity and financial affairs, the main group of users usually being identified as those who have a known or potential investment commitment with it – i.e. investors and creditors (although others such as employees and government must also be recognized). All are concerned in some way with making decisions in relation to their interests in the entity. For example, the 'investor' (be he owner, lender or creditor) requires information pertaining to his future returns from the investment. In particular, the owner would need information with which to predict future distributions from the entity; and the lender and creditor would need information with which to predict the ability of the entity to repay amounts due to them. The question therefore is whether or not an income-orientated reporting system satisfies these goals – i.e. whether or not measures of historic cost or current value based income are useful to the 'investor' when he is attempting to predict future returns to him.

Distributions, for example, appear to require an assessment of two factors – the availability of distributable income, and the availability of cash to satisfy the eventual payments. The first factor is the familiar legal one of ensuring that distributions are not repayments of capital; and the second factor is the commonsense one of financial prudence, depending to a considerable extent on the need for the entity to retain liquid resources to maintain and expand its existing operations. So far as the legality of dividends is concerned, there does not appear to be an absolute need for income figures to ensure the appropriate mainte-nance of subscribed capital. Indeed, this particular point can be established by means of relatively simple statements of cash move-ments since the original subscription – distributions being payable only out of cash generated from sources other than capital receipts. In addition, statements of measured income appear to be an irrelevance for purposes of financial prudence when distributing, because the key factor is the availability of cash rather than the availability of so-called distributable income. Thus, from the point of view of assessing possible dividends, it appears that the availability of cash from operational or trading sources is the most significant matter, and that periodic in-come, although traditionally used in this exercise, is not as relevant as its past use in this context indicates.

The information needs of lenders and creditors also appear to centre on the cash position of the entity – i.e. the availability of cash resources to enable it to meet its relevant interest and repayment commitments. In this respect, income does not appear to be a significant factor in helping lenders and creditors to predict future liquidity positions. Rather, it is the cash-generating potential of the company which is likely to interest them, not its income-generating potential. The finan-cial information needs of employees is an increasingly important topic. Concerned about wage claims and employment prospects, they too look for information to enable them to predict. In this sense, it could be argued that periodic income of the entity is not particularly useful – income does not necessarily generate the cash required for meeting wage claims and for providing continuity of employment. Indeed, it can positively mislead in this respect.

Finally, the information requirements of a further group of users of financial information should be noted – i.e. the Inland Revenue. The entire system of business taxation in Britain and elsewhere is based on an assessment of periodic income. Historic cost accounting income has been used for many years as the basis for computing such taxation liabilities. It would therefore appear to be the case that, subject to radical changes in the basis of computing tax, income must remain of primary importance in this respect – despite the faults and problems associated with its use in other areas. But it must be stated that taxation of entities need not necessarily be based on their measured income. It is simply convention and habit that supports the present practice.

## An alternative to income

The foregoing remarks do not reflect well on the concept of income as it relates to the business entity: it is subject to a great deal of variation in both its conception and practice; its measurement is open to criticism; its meaning is imprecise and it does not appear to be entirely appropriate to the economic factors it is intended to symbolize; nor does it appear to be obviously relevant to the majority of persons who may be assumed to be using it. As the main objective of accounting is to provide financial information which is relevant to the needs of its users, it is appropriate to look a little more closely at this point and, particularly, to see whether there is an alternative form of financial report which may eventually supplant the income statement.

The problem with reporting systems which concentrate on measures of income is that they tend inevitably to focus accountants' attention on the very significant problems associated with income determination and asset valuation. In other words, there is the danger that other relevant forms of financial reporting may be neglected, thus placing income reporting in a place of prominence which is not fully deserved or justified. The purpose of this section, therefore, is to look at one alternative which appears to have as much, if not more, relevance to investors and others interested in the financial affairs of companies – the system of so-called cash flow reporting.[4]

In the previous section dealing with the information needs of owners and others, it was suggested that all such groups, despite their differing interests in the business entity, were concerned generally with its future development and progress and particularly with its ability to pay wages, interest and distributions and to repay liabilities, over what could be a considerable period of time. This would further suggest that such persons require information which reflects these factors. The question posed is whether the traditional income statement, together with its supporting balance sheet, is sufficient for this purpose.

The income statement and the balance sheet, whatever the valuation basis used, cannot be expected to reveal the full picture of how the entity is developing and progressing over time. The income statement portrays a periodic measure of operational activity, and the balance sheet reflects the entity's resultant financial position at one point in time. The inevitable information gap which exists because of the limitations of these two statements has resulted in an increasing use in recent years of a further financial report – i.e. the funds statement, which is intended to show periodic changes in the sources of finance available to the entity as well as the ways in which the resultant funds have been employed by it. It is this type of dynamic report which appears to have relevance to a person assessing and predicting the financial progress of an individual business over time. However, funds flow reports contain one very significant limiting factor – they are based upon the concept of income and its supporting system of allocation accounting.

Thus, the flow of funds depicted in such statements contains all the measurement faults and problems associated with income determination. Despite this problem, the concept of reporting on the flow of entity funds appears to have great relevance to owners and others, and should be pursued further – particularly its adaptation to a cash basis.

There is one economic factor which is crucial to a proper assessment of the distribution potential, etc. of the entity, and that is its capacity to survive – indeed, it could be argued that survival should be the primary business objective. If the entity does not survive over the long term, there will be no flow of distributions, no payment of wages and interest, and no repayment of loans and other amounts due. Therefore, it can be argued that owners and other interested parties require information which enables them to assess and predict the development and progress of the individual business entity over time: its capacity to survive, and its capacity to pay its distribution, wage, interest, and repayment commitments.

Ideally, the information required should be expressed as a flow of funds in order to reflect these factors. In particular, it should also be measuring the one resource which indicates progress, survival and the ability to provide returns on investments – i.e. cash. A business cannot survive, progress, repay loans and other debts, or distribute without cash. The ability of the entity to generate sufficient cash for these purposes appears to be of crucial interest to owners and others, and this has been hinted at already in the previous section dealing with information needs.

Such a system would add a new dimension to financial reporting, showing sources and uses of cash over a period of time. The cash flows could be segregated to disclose those which evolve from trading operations, financial activities, long-term investment, and so on. The statements could be supported by other statements disclosing non-cash transactions, such as in acquisitions and mergers with other companies, which could have a significant bearing on the capacity of the entity to survive. They could also be subject to audit, in much the same way as for traditional financial statements, not only to verify their adequacy but also to remove any suspicion that company management may be manipulating the figures by delaying or accelerating cash movements. It could also be recommended, for the above reason and because of the need to disclose a sufficient trend of figures, that several years' data be reported. Additionally, and in order to minimize the criticism that past flows may not be repeated in the future, forecast data could also be reported. The relevance of this information to owners and others appears to outweigh by far its inevitable subjectiveness. The reporting of at least one year's forecast data should not present insuperable problems, because it is information which management should have available in any case.

**Illustration 27 A cash flow accounting statement**

| Cash flows | Period | | | | |
|---|---|---|---|---|---|
| | $t_0-t_1$ £ | $t_1-t_2$ £ | $t_2-t_3$ £ | $t_3-t_4$ £ | Total £ |
| *Inflows* | | | | | |
| Operating cash flow | 2,000 | 2,500 | 1,700 | — | 6,200 |
| Capital received | 6,200 | — | — | — | 6,200 |
| Sale of shop and van | — | — | — | 10,400[a] | 10,400 |
| Decrease in cash balance | — | — | — | 6,200[b] | —[c] |
| | 8,200 | 2,500 | 1,700 | 16,600 | 22,800 |
| *Outflows* | | | | | |
| Purchase of shop and van | 6,200[d] | — | — | — | 6,200 |
| Distribution | — | — | — | 16,600 | 16,600 |
| Increase in cash balance | 2,000[e] | 2,500[f] | 1,700[g] | — | —[c] |
| | 8,200 | 2,500 | 1,700 | 16,600 | 22,800 |

(a) £10,300 + 100; (b) £6,200 − 0; (c) £6,200 − 6,200; (d) £5,000 + 1,200; (e) £2,000 − 0; (f) £4,500 − 2,000; (g) £6,200 − 4,500.

Illustration 27 is based on the business situation data used throughout Chapters 4 to 10 inclusive – i.e. a business opened at $t_0$ with the purchase of a motor van for £1,200 and a shop for £5,000; cash operating surpluses before depreciation were £2,000 (period $t_0-t_1$), £2,500 (period $t_1-t_2$) and £1,700 (period $t_2-t_3$); realization of the van and shop immediately after $t_3$ was for £100 and £10,300 respectively when business operations ceased, and the first and final distribution was made to the owner. The illustration reveals in outline only the cash flow accounting statement which could be derived from these data. It would, of course, require further disclosure to support the brevity of the stated figures. However, it should be noted that it is the first and only illustration of the business situation used throughout this text which is devoid of the application of valuation procedures, accounting principles, and subjective judgements. As such, it is the least biased of all accounting statements described in the book.

The above outline cash flow statement reports on realized cash flows only. As such, it avoids disclosure of an income measure and a supporting statement of financial position. This should not be surprising as it was conceived originally as an alternative to the reporting of income. However, it is possible to combine the reporting of realized cash flows with that of unrealized cash flows. By doing this, the reporting system brings together cash flow accounting and net realizable value accounting.[5] A measure of realizable income can be produced which is described as a combination of realized and unrealized cash flows. It can be supported by a net realizable value-based balance sheet. It is important to note that this is a system designed to reveal actual and potential cash flows. It is therefore an alternative view of the realizable income and value model, and incorporates the various benefits of the latter.[6] Assuming the following net realizable values for the van and the shop at the stated dates: at $t_1$ van £850, shop £5,700; at $t_2$, van £350, shop £7,000; and at $t_3$, van £100, shop £9,500; and also using the data given for Illustration 27, the undernoted statement of realizable cash flows can be produced. It would be supported by a Statement of Realized Cash Flow (as in Illustration 27) and a balance sheet on a net realizable value basis (as in Illustration 16).

**Illustration 28 Statement of realizable cash flows**

| | Period | | | | |
|---|---|---|---|---|---|
| | $t_0 - t_1$ £ | $t_1 - t_2$ £ | $t_2 - t_3$ £ | $t_3 - t_4$ £ | Total £ |
| *Realized cash flows* | | | | | |
| Operating cash flow | 2,000 | 2,500 | 1,700 | — | 6,200 |
| Realization of shop | — | — | — | 800[(a)] | 800 |
| *Unrealized cash flows* Change of value of: | | | | | |
| van | (350) | (500)[(c)] | (250)[(d)] | — | (1,100) |
| shop | 700[(c)] | 1,300[(f)] | 2,500[(g)] | — | 4,500 |
| | 350 | 800 | 2,250 | — | 3,400 |
| *Realizable cash flows* | 2,350 | 3,300 | 3,950 | 800 | 10,400 |

(a) £10,300 − 9,500; (b) £850 − £1,200; (c) £350 − 850; (d) £100 − £350; (e) £5,700 − 5,000; (f) £7,500 − 5,700; (g) £9,500 − 7,000.

The figures for realizable cash flows are identical to those of realizable income (Illustration 16). The difference is in the way in which they have been described. Those above are stated as cash flows; those in the realizable income model are disclosed as price variations.

The arguments for a system of cash flow reporting are numerous, and appear significant enough to warrant a little more attention than they have been given hitherto.

**1** It is the generation of use of cash which enables the entity to survive; investment in it, whatever its form, depends entirely on its capacity to accumulate and apply cash in the most efficient and productive ways possible.

**2** Thus, although it may be argued that the income of the entity is symbolic of its success, and therefore of its survival, it is no more than a symbol. Cash is the underlying economic success factor, income is not; and cash flow reporting therefore concentrates on the reality rather than the traditional symbol of entity success and survival.

**3** Cash is an economic factor which most persons in a developed society understand, through their day-to-day affairs. Income, on the other hand, is not, for it has developed far beyond the relatively simple surplus accounting generally associated with matching revenues and costs. Cash flow reporting attempts to avoid the considerable conceptual and practical measurement problems wich beset income determination and asset valuation.

**4** The prediction of future distributions, loan repayments, creditor payments, and so on appear to be far more strongly related to cash changes and situations than to periodic income. This further suggests a de-emphasizing of income as the primary financial reporting concept.

**5** Cash flow reporting appears to satisfy the need to supply owners and others with stewardship-orientated information as well as with decision-orientated information. By reducing judgements in this type of financial report, management can report factually on its stewardship function, whilst at the same time disclosing date of use in the decision making process. In other words, cash flow reporting eliminates the somewhat artificial segregation of stewardship and decision making information.

**6** Comparability, both inter- and intra-firm, is considerably enhanced by cash flow reporting; not only are data expressed in the same terms, free of the abuses of valuation and allocation accounting, but they can be compared with prior expectations if forecast data are also disclosed.

### Conclusion
The primary intention of this chapter has been to explore and analyse the complex nature of the income concept, which has dominated, and still does, the present-day system of business financial reporting. The concept can be criticized on many grounds, sufficiently to suggest that it should not be regarded as the only major indicator of business entity progress. Thus, it would be foolish to argue against it completely; to do so would be to argue against the many years of constant and, presumably, successful use made of it by countless persons in the area of financial management. Indeed, simply because of the present tax structure, the income of business entities cannot be neglected. The defects attributable to income therefore warrant consideration of other forms of financial report which appear as relevant to the needs of owners and others. In this respect, cash flow reports appear worthy of a great deal of attention.

## References

(See page 180 for Selected Bibliography)

1. J. R. Hicks, *Value and Capital*, Clarendon Press, 2nd Edition, 1946, pp. 180–1.
2. S. H. Frankel, *Economic Impact on Underdeveloped Societies*, Basil Blackwell, 1953, p. 55.
3. D. Solomons, 'Economic and Accounting Concepts of Income', *Accounting Review*, July 1961, p. 382.
4. For further details, see T.A. Lee, 'Cash Flow Accounting and Cash Flow Reporting', in M. Bromwich and A. Hopwood (eds.), *Essays in British Accounting Research*, Pitman, 1981, pp. 63–78.
5. See T.A. Lee, 'Reporting Cash Flows and Net Realizable Values', *Accounting and Business Research*, Spring 1981, pp. 163–70.
6. A full description is provided in T.A. Lee, *Cash Flow Accounting*, Van Nostrand Reinhold (UK), 1984.

# Selected bibliography

The footnote references at the end of each chapter will provide the reader with additional material to supplement the text. However, they do not represent a deliberate selection of writings which ought to be studied to provide the reader with an adequate knowledge and understanding of each topic. With this in mind, the undernoted items have been chosen to provide such a knowledge and understanding. They do not, of course, represent a complete study course but they should provide the reader with a useful start to a journey well worth pursuing.

The writings have been selected on the basis of their readability, relevance and significance to the study of income and value measurement. They have been classified into appropriate groupings in order to aid the teacher and student commencing their 'paper chase'.

### History of the subject
In order to provide a background to a proper study of income and value measurement problems, it is essential to put the latter within their historical context. This helps to identify the long-lived issues and also the major contributors.

P. Rosenfield, 'A History of Inflation Accounting', *Journal of Accountancy,* September 1981, pp.95–126.

G. Whittington, 'The British Contribution to Income Theory', in M. Bromwich and A. Hopwood (eds.), *Essays in British Accounting Research,* Pitman, 1981, pp.1–29.

G. Whittington, 'The European Contribution to Inflation Accounting', *Congress Papers,* European Accounting Association, 1984, pp.24–42.

The above writings provide a full coverage of contributions from Australia, the United Kingdom, the United States and Continental Europe. In particular, they focus attention on the origins of income and value issues in the early 1900s.

**The classics**

It is vital for every student of income and value measurement to read classic contributions to the area. These are listed below with relevant comments. The first part of the 1900s saw the publication of several texts which formed the basis for the present interest in current value accounting and general price-level adjustments.

J. B. Canning, *The Economics of Accountancy,* Arno Press, 1978 reprint.

K. MacNeal, *Truth in Accounting,* Scholars Book Co., 1970 reprint.

H. W. Sweeney, *Stabilized Accounting,* Holt Rinehart and Winston, 1964 reprint.

Canning and MacNeal consider the relevance of mixed value models. Sweeney, on the other hand, deals with the issue of general price-level adjustments related to replacement cost accounting. Each text has been a considerable platform for the following contributions written in the 1960s.

R. J. Chambers, *Accounting, Evaluation and Economic Behaviour,* Scholars Book Co., 1974 reprint.

E. O. Edwards and P. W. Bell, *The Theory and Measurement of Business Income,* University of California Press, 1961.

R. R. Sterling, *Theory of the Measurement of Enterprise Income,* Scholars Book Co., 1979 reprint.

Edwards and Bell advocate the use of replacement costs whereas Chambers and Sterling provide cases for net realizable values. Each is a considerable argument for the income and value model concerned, and has had a significant influence on several generations of students.

**Collections of writings**

The above suggested readings can be supplemented usefully by items from a number of well-known collections of writings. The following volumes provide a general coverage of the issues and models concerned:

W. T. Baxter and S. Davidson (eds.), *Studies in Accounting,* Institute of Chartered Accountants in England and Wales, 1977.

R. H. Parker and G. C. Harcourt (eds.), *Readings in the Concept and Measurement of Income,* Cambridge University Press, 1969.

R. R. Sterling (ed.), *Asset Valuation and Income Determination—a Consideration of the Alternatives,* Scholars Book Co., 1971.

R. R. Sterling and A. L. Thomas (eds.), *Accounting for a Simplified Firm Owning Depreciable Assets,* Scholars Book Co., 1979.

Studies of particular issues can be found in the following further collections:

G. W. Dean and M. C. Wells, *Current Cost Accounting : Identifying the Issues,* ICRA and University of Lancaster, 1982.

G. W. Dean and M. C. Wells, *The Case for Continuously Contemporary Accounting,* Garland Press, 1984.

R. R. Sterling and K. W. Lemke, *Maintenance of Capital : Financial Versus Physical,* Scholars Book Co., 1982.

### Specific writings

Readers may supplement their reading of individual chapters in this text by the following recommended writings:

*In relation to Chapters 1 and 2:*

W. H. Beaver and J. S. Demski, 'The Nature of Income Measurement', *Accounting Review,* January 1979, pp.38–46.

M. Bromwich and M. C. Wells, 'The Usefulness of a Measure of Wealth', *Abacus,* December 1983, pp.119–29.

R. S. Gynther, 'Capital Maintenance, Price Changes, and Profit Determination', *Accounting Review,* October 1970, pp.712–30.

K. Shwayder, 'The Capital Maintenance Rule and the Net Asset Valuation Rule', *Accounting Review,* April 1969, pp.304–16.

R. R. Sterling, 'Relevant Financial Reporting in an Age of Price Changes', *Journal of Accountancy,* February 1975, pp.42–51.

*In relation to Chapter 3:*

M. Bromwich, 'The Use of Present Value Valuation Models in Published Accounting Reports', *Accounting Review,* July 1977, pp.587–96.

H. Bierman and S. Davidson, 'The Income Concept–Value Increment or Earnings Predictor?', *Accounting Review,* April 1969, pp.239–46.

K. V. Peasnell, 'The Present Value Concept in Financial Reporting', *Journal of Business Finance and Accounting,* Summer 1977, pp.153–68.

R. W. Scapens, 'A Neoclassical Measure of Profit', *Accounting Review,* April 1978, pp.448–69.

K. Shwayder, 'A Critique of Economic Income as an Accounting Concept', *Abacus,* August 1967, pp.23–35.

*In relation to Chapter 4:*

R. N. Anthony, 'A Case for Historical Costs', *Harvard Business Review,* November–December 1976, pp.69–79.

E. Kohler, 'Why Not Retain Historic Cost?', *Journal of Accountancy,* October 1963, pp.35–41.

C. T. Horngren, 'How Should We Interpret the Realization Concept?', *Accounting Review,* April 1965, pp.323–33.

R. R. Sterling, 'Conservatism: The Fundamental Principle of Valuation in Traditional Accounting', *Abacus,* December 1967, pp.109–32.

I. Tilley, 'A Critique of Historical Record Accounting', *Accounting and Business Research,* Summer 1975, pp.185–97.

*In relation to Chapter 5:*

N. M. Bedford and J. C. McKeown, 'A Comparative Analysis of Net Realizable Value and Replacement Costing,' *Accounting Review,* April 1972, pp.333–8.

M. Bromwich, 'Asset Valuation with Imperfect Markets', *Accounting and Business Research,* Autumn 1975, pp.242–53.

R. L. Matthews, 'Income, Price Changes and the Valuation Controversy in Accounting', *Accounting Review,* July 1968, pp.509–16.

P. Rosenfield, 'The Confusion Between General Price-level Restatement and Current Value Accounting', *Journal of Accountancy,* October 1972, pp.63–8.

R. R. Sterling, 'Decision Orientated Financial Accounting', *Accounting and Business Research,* Summer 1972, pp.198–208.

*In relation to Chapter 6:*

P. W. Bell, 'CVA, CCA and CoCoA : How Fundamental are the Differences?', *Accounting Theory Monograph 1,* Australian Research Foundation, 1982.

E. O. Edwards, 'The State of Current Value Accounting', *Accounting Review,* April 1975, pp.235–45.

K. P. Gee and K. V. Peasnell, 'A Pragmatic Defence of Replacement Cost', *Accounting and Business Research,* Autumn 1976, pp.242–9.

P. Prakash and S. Sunder, 'The Case against Separation of Current Operating Profit and Holding Gain', *Accounting Review,* January 1979, pp.1–22.

R. A. Samuelson, 'Should Replacement–Cost Changes Be Included in Income?', *Accounting Review,* April 1980, pp.254–68.

*In relation to Chapter 7:*

R. J. Chambers, 'Continuously Contemporary Accounting : Misunderstandings and Misrepresentations', *Abacus,* December 1976, pp.137–51.

L. A. Friedman, 'An Exit – Price Income Statement', *Accounting Review,* January 1978, pp.18 – 30.

S. J. Gray and M. C. Wells, 'Asset Values and Ex Post Income', *Accounting and Business Research,* Summer 1973, pp.163 – 7.

R. R Sterling, 'Costs (Historical Versus Current) Versus Exit Values', *Abacus,* December 1981, pp.93 – 129.

D. W. Vickrey, 'A Commentary on the Addition of Current Price Values', *Journal of Business Finance and Accounting,* Winter 1978, pp.413 – 23.

*In relation to Chapter 8:*

H. C. Edey, 'Deprival Value and Financial Accounting', in H. C. Edey and B. S. Yamey (eds.), *Debits, Credits, Finance and Profits,* Sweet and Maxwell, 1974, pp.75 – 83.

R. Ma, 'Value to the Owner Revisited', *Abacus,* December 1976, pp.159 – 65.

G. Macdonald, 'Deprival Value : Its Use and Abuse', *Accounting and Business Research,* Autumn 1974, pp.263 – 9.

E. Stamp, 'Income and Value Determination and Changing Price-Levels : an Essay Towards a Theory', *Accountant's Magazine,* June 1971, pp.277 – 92.

H. Yoshida, 'Value to the Firm and the Asset Measurement Problem', *Abacus,* June 1973, pp.16 – 21.

*In relation to Chapter 9:*

A. Barton, 'An Analysis of Business Income Concepts', *Occasional Paper 7,* ICRA, 1975.

J. S. Cook and O. J. Holzmann, 'Current Cost and Present Value in Income Theory', *Accounting Review,* October 1976, pp.778 – 87.

S. H. Penman, 'What Net Asset Value? — an Extension of a Familiar Debate', *Accounting Review,* April 1970, pp.333 – 46.

L. Revsine, 'On the Correspondence Between Replacement Cost Income and Economic Income', *Accounting Review,* July 1970, pp.513 – 23.

F. K. Wright, 'The Relationship Between Present Value and Value to the Owner', *Journal of Business Finance,* Summer 1973, pp.19 – 25.

*In relation to Chapter 10:*

R. S. Gynther, 'Why Use General Purchasing Power?', *Accounting and Business Research,* Spring 1974, pp.141 – 57.

R. Ma and M. C. Miller, 'Inflation and the Current Value Illusion', *Accounting and Business Research,* Autumn 1976, pp.250 – 63.

R. L. Matthews, 'Price-Level Changes and Useless Information', *Journal of Accounting Research,* Spring 1965, pp.133 – 55.

M. Moonitz, 'Price-Level Accounting and Scales of Measurement', *Accounting Review,* July 1970, pp.465 – 75.

L. Revsine and J. J. Weygandt, 'Accounting for Inflation : The Controversy', *Journal of Accountancy,* October 1974, pp.72 – 8.

*In relation to Chapter 11:*

L. G. Eckel, 'Arbitrary and Incorrigible Allocations', *Accounting Review,* October 1976, pp.764 – 77.

G. H. Lawson, 'Cash-Flow Accounting', *Accountant,* 28 October 1971, pp.386 – 9 and 4 November 1971, pp.620 – 22.

T. A. Lee, 'A Case for Cash Flow Reporting', *Journal of Business Finance,* Summer 1972, pp.27 – 36.

M. Moonitz, 'Should We Discard the Income Concept?', *Accounting Review,* April 1962, pp.175 – 80.

B. A. Rutherford, 'The Interpretation of Cash Flow Reports and the Other Allocation Problem', *Abacus,* June 1982, pp.40 – 49.

# Index